I0605062

sit Christian Art Gifts, Inc., at www.christianartgifts.com.

*ne Welcoming Home: A 52-Week Devotional Guide to Showing Hospitality for God's Glory*

ublished by Christian Art Gifts, Inc., Bloomingdale, IL, USA.



he author is represented by Barbara Roose, Books & Such Literary Management,
ww.booksandsuch.com.

irst edition 2025.

esigned by Christian Art Gifts, Inc.

Cover and interior photography used under license from Alexandria Hinders Creative at
lexandriahinderscreative.com. Supplemental interior images used under license from
shutterstock.com.



Most Christian Art titles may be purchased at bulk discounts by churches, non-profits,
and corporations. For more information, please email SpecialMarkets@cagifts.com.

ISBN 978-1-63952-898-1

Printed in China.

31 30 29 28 27 26
11 10 9 8 7 6 5 4 3 2

# The *Welcoming* HOME

A 52-Week Devotional Guide to Showing Hospitality for God's Glory

HILARY BERNSTEIN

# *Table of Contents*

# *Introduction*

*Welcome*! No other word in the English language may seem so inviting, kind, and inclusive. When you feel welcomed, you know that someone is truly glad to see you. You're received with joy, and you feel like you matter.

Welcomes are wonderful because the unquestionable truth is that you *do* matter. Since every person is created in the image of God, every person matters. Everyone deserves a welcome. It doesn't matter what your age or stage is, what your strengths or weaknesses are, or how much or little you accomplish or offer to others; you are worthy of being welcomed.

Yet, in order to be welcomed, you need to be willing to come. The only way you'll be able to welcome guests is for you to invite them and for them to accept your invitation.

The necessity of a generous welcome to absolutely everyone was made clear by Jesus Christ. Throughout His Word, the Lord Himself reveals that He's ready to welcome all. In His time on earth, Jesus extended invitation after invitation to welcome everyone:

- Jesus invited people to "*Come*, follow me." (Matthew 4:19; emphasis mine)
- He offered, "*Come* to me, *all* you who are weary and burdened, and I will give you rest." (Matthew 11:28; emphasis mine)

  And Jesus promised:

> "I am the bread of life. *Whoever comes to me* will never go hungry, and whoever believes in me will never be thirsty. But as I told you, you have seen me and still you do not believe. All those the Father gives me will come to me, and *whoever comes to me* I will never drive away. For I have come down from heaven not to do my will but to do the will of him who sent me. And this is the will of him who sent me, that I shall lose none of all those he has given me, but raise them up at the last day. For my Father's will is that everyone who looks to the Son and believes in him shall have eternal life, and I will raise them up at the last day." (John 6:35–40; emphasis mine)

These weren't requests intended for one time only. Jesus extends the same offers to you and me today. Just as Jesus offers His invitation and welcomes His followers with the gift of eternal life, you and I can reach out to others every day with a genuine invitation into our lives and a warm welcome into our homes. Who knows? Perhaps by welcoming others into our lives with transparency and kindness we can begin to point them to Christ and His welcome in an authentic way.

As we choose to welcome others, it's important to remember that only one defining characteristic or motivation is necessary: Loving others as Christ loves you should be the distinguishing factor in the life of a believer in Christ.

The truly great news is that loving others is at the heart of welcoming others. While you certainly can welcome others with your words and your actions—and being welcomed with a smile, friendly greeting, or a hug is wonderful!—intentionally choosing to use your home as a place to welcome others becomes a powerfully tangible expression of love.

Instead of looking at your home only as a shelter from the weather, what if you began to see it as a way to provide shelter from the storms of this life?

Rather than using your home to escape from the demands and pressures of the world, what if you open up your haven to *others* as a way to replenish or revive their spirits?

And instead of thinking of your home as a place you need to organize, decorate, keep clean, and maintain, what if you considered these basic chores as ways to create a place to nourish and nurture other image bearers, from the people who already live in your home to the people who come for a visit?

As tempted as you may feel to search for a bunch of quick fixes to create a home that looks or feels more welcoming for others, this is a process that could and should take time. Yes, you eventually may need to change things around your home, but, more importantly, you need to step back and focus on changing your heart. You'll need a lot of prayerful consideration to make meaningful changes that will last in your home and your life.

*The Welcoming Home* is designed to help you slow down and ponder this process. Take your time as you consider how you might glorify the Lord through your thoughts, actions, attitudes, and home. Slow down to pray, asking Him to guide and help you. Search your heart to identify ways you could or should change. It may feel tempting to rush through just to mark things off of your mental to-do list, but by taking things slowly, you'll be able to get to the heart of hospitality. You'll experience truly compelling motivation to welcome others.

While a common current focus on welcoming is based on impressing and entertaining guests, biblical hospitality takes a radically different approach. As you become more welcoming, not only in your attitude and relationships with others but also with the way you share your home with them, you reflect the true heart of hospitality. Welcoming isn't about the tastiest recipes, most spectacular homes, or stellar activities. It's about investing in others by being present, genuinely interested in their lives, and willing to give your time, energy, and focus to them. In short, welcoming revolves around loving others well, as Christ commanded.

This book includes fifty-two devotions centered on what the Bible teaches about welcome and hospitality. You may choose to slow down and focus on one devotion a week. As you read and pray about the biblical truth in each portion, you should take the time to make any necessary adjustments in your life and home.

May this book be a good resource to center your heart and mind on the blessing and gift that welcoming can become for you and others. Resist the urge to rush through and skip the practical exercises. As you commit to doing the work, you'll discover changes in your heart and home.

## *What can you expect?*

- Each day begins with Scripture to consider, followed by a devotional thought that will help you process what you've read in the Bible. A prayer wraps everything up as you trust the Lord to work in your life and home.
- A "Think It Over" section includes several questions for you to ask yourself and spend time pondering. Because you don't have to share your answers with anyone, take your time and be truthful! Prayerfully consider each of these questions. Let the Lord reveal what's going on in your heart and mind.
- Once you've honestly considered your responses, a "Put It into Practice" section includes one to two personal challenges to help you live a more welcoming, hospitable life.

- Finally, a "Home Work" section helps you practically prepare your home for guests. At its core, hospitality is a heart issue. It involves you and your willingness to get to know and bless others by opening your home. Details and surroundings aren't important. However, sometimes you feel a lot more comfortable if your house feels ready for company. In fact, getting our homes ready for guests can be one of the top reasons many people choose *not* to host—it simply feels like a lot of work. By keeping up with your home and making it company-ready, you can feel a lot more prepared when you make an invitation and open your home with a heart of hospitality.

As you read and pray through *The Welcoming Home*, work through the assignments, and put principles into practice, may you notice a difference in your life, your home, and your relationships. May the Lord work in mighty ways as you partner with Him to love others well simply by opening your door in a warm welcome.

# *Welcome!*

From something you do to a way that you feel, *welcome* is a word of many uses and purposes.

According to the *Merriam-Webster Dictionary*, the word *welcome* can be used as a verb when you hospitably greet someone out of courtesy: "This afternoon, I'm welcoming my friends over for lunch."

Welcome is also a noun, a cordial reception when someone arrives. For example, "My hostess thoughtfully gave me a warm welcome."

Welcome can be used as an adjective in a variety of ways. You might be received by someone with gladness: "I always was welcome in Grandma's kitchen." Or you could receive something with pleasure: "The finish line was a welcome sight." Or you might be permitted to do something: "You are welcome to come over any time."

As a greeting, welcome can be an interjection: "Welcome!"

And "You're welcome" is the most common response to "Thank you."

However you choose to use *welcome*, it bubbles over with kind intention. Think of the way words like *courteous*, *cordial*, *gladness*, and *pleasure* are associated with *welcome*. There's no grumbling or complaining, no drudgery or obligation. A true welcome is filled with warmth and good intentions. It brings joy and calms the nerves of both the giver and the receiver.

As you consider the kind of welcome that overflows with peace and pleasure, courtesy and kindness, consider the welcomes described in the Bible. Scriptural accounts share how some people welcomed with gladness while others chose not to welcome at all. After you read each of the following devotions, ponder what your own hospitality and welcomes look like. Consider how you could better reflect the love of the Lord by the way you welcome your guests.

WELCOME

# Welcoming with Gladness

*Jesus entered Jericho and was passing through. A man was there by the name of Zacchaeus; he was a chief tax collector and was wealthy. He wanted to see who Jesus was, but because he was short he could not see over the crowd. So he ran ahead and climbed a sycamore-fig tree to see him, since Jesus was coming that way.*

*When Jesus reached the spot, he looked up and said to him, "Zacchaeus, come down immediately. I must stay at your house today." So he came down at once and welcomed him gladly.*

*All the people saw this and began to mutter, "He has gone to be the guest of a sinner."*

*But Zacchaeus stood up and said to the Lord, "Look, Lord! Here and now I give half of my possessions to the poor, and if I have cheated anybody out of anything, I will pay back four times the amount."*

*Jesus said to him, "Today salvation has come to this house, because this man, too, is a son of Abraham. For the Son of Man came to seek and to save the lost."*

LUKE 19:1–10

What kind of a welcomer are you? Do you typically light up with joy when you see someone else? Are you slow to warm? Do you stay calm and collected? Are you friendly but reserved? Outright grouchy? Bubbling with happiness? If someone says she is coming to your home, do you tend to respond with happiness or try to make excuses? Or does your response depend completely on the day you're asked or the season of life you're in or what's on your mind?

Since Jesus' earthly ministry involved frequent travel from town to town, He and His disciples experienced a lot of different welcomes. They met a lot of people and visited a lot of homes. In their journeys, they didn't stick to themselves, and they didn't stay secluded with the religious elite.

Rather, Jesus took the initiative to go everywhere throughout the region—Jewish territories and Gentile territories. As He went, He talked to everyone—rich and poor, religious and pagan, well and sick.

When Jesus got to Jericho, He met Zacchaeus, a chief tax collector. Since tax collectors were shunned by much of society, onlookers were shocked not only that Jesus talked with this tax collector but also that He invited Himself to the house of Zacchaeus.

Zacchaeus might have been shocked too, but the unanticipated visit from Jesus touched his heart in such a way that he responded from a transformed perspective.

Once Jesus said that He must stay at Zacchaeus's house, Zacchaeus got busy immediately. First, he left his observation spot in the tree. Second, he welcomed Jesus gladly. Third, the heart of Zacchaeus was changed so much that he chose to give half of his possessions to the poor and repay anyone he cheated—not just an even repayment, but four times that amount.

Simply meeting Jesus radically changed Zacchaeus's heart and mind in a moment. Here was a man who readily admitted that he was wealthy and that his wealth wasn't always acquired in an honest and upright way. Yet when Zacchaeus gladly welcomed Jesus to his home (and presumably his life), he was ready to show his devotion by giving half of his possessions to the poor. He felt compelled to generously pay back what he might have taken dishonestly.

Just as Zacchaeus radically changed for the better after he had gladly welcomed Jesus, your life will be transformed when you choose to gladly welcome Jesus. Watch the way your former loves and passions pale in comparison to Him. Watch the way generosity springs up in your heart until you can't help but share with those around you. And watch the way you'll be able to tune out what any naysayers might say about you and listen to the Son of God's clear call to freedom and identity in Him.

*Lord Jesus, You are the one who rescues. You are the one who transforms. I praise You for the miraculous way You work and move in the hearts of people You call to Yourself. What You do is amazing! Just as Zacchaeus welcomed You to his life and home with joy, I want to welcome You to my life. May my heart be so tethered to You that I turn from my sinful ways and glorify You with a warm, glad welcome. In Your name I pray, amen.*

## Think It Over

- How could you improve the way you welcome people? What would make your welcomes warmer?
- Have you watched Jesus completely transform someone's life? What was the person like before Christ stepped in? What was the person like after he or she gladly welcomed Jesus?
- If one of your personal weaknesses is money, whether it involves earning it, saving it, or spending it, what can you do to bring your finances under Christ's lordship?
- Zacchaeus was moved to obedience once Jesus told him to come down from the tree to be an unexpected host. Like Zacchaeus, are you mentally prepared to drop everything to host an unexpected guest?

## Put It into Practice

- Zacchaeus got so excited about Jesus that he was ready to give half his possessions to the poor. Take a moment to look around your home. What can you give to the poor? Gather it up and find a recipient or a local donation center.
- Zacchaeus was ready at a moment's notice to welcome Jesus to his home. Are you ready to make a last-minute invitation? Is your home ready to welcome people at the spur of the moment?

## Home Work

One of the first things your guests see when they approach your home is your entryway. What does yours look like? How inviting is it? How distracting or off-putting is it? Does it look like you're ready to welcome people into your home? Take time this week to straighten up and clean your entryway. Yours is unique to your home, so your tasks may include sweeping the floor, cleaning a porch light, or wiping off a mailbox. If you can add something cheerful and inviting, like a potted plant or a seating area, take time to make an update!

# What Your Welcome Says About You

*When you enter a town and are welcomed, eat what is offered to you. Heal the sick who are there and tell them, "The kingdom of God has come near to you." But when you enter a town and are not welcomed, go into its streets and say, "Even the dust of your town we wipe from our feet as a warning to you. Yet be sure of this: The kingdom of God has come near."*

Luke 10:8–11

Have you ever stopped to consider what your welcome reveals about who you are? First impressions mean a lot. And the way you treat someone, from the look on your face to the tone of your voice, speaks volumes. Often, you can sense if a stranger is welcoming or standoffish by his or her welcome.

When people meet you for the first time at your home, the way you welcome them can completely set the tone for much of your visit or even your relationship.

Think about a time in your life when you met a stranger for the first time at his or her home. What kind of welcome did this person give? Was he or she friendly and inquisitive? Or unfriendly, aloof, or distracted?

Like it or not, the way you meet someone for the first time can impact your relationship, positively or negatively. That initial impression may not make or break your relationship, but it certainly affects how others view you. Especially when it's at your home, your warm welcome could set the stage for a friendly, positive relationship. Or, if you're in the middle of a bad day and you're dealing with all sorts of chaos and confusion, it will take a while to move past that impression. It's possible to turn an unfavorable impression around, but it might be difficult. And it might take a while.

Just as the kind of welcome that you *give* others matters, Jesus taught His disciples to pay attention to the kind of welcome they might *receive*. Sometimes His disciples would be welcomed into homes, but some people turned them away. And sometimes entire towns would welcome the disciples, while other towns chose to not welcome them.

For Jesus, a welcome made a huge difference. If a town welcomed His disciples by offering them food, Jesus encouraged His disciples to heal the sick and to tell the residents that the kingdom of God had come near. When you think about it, He offered a lot of blessings in return for a welcome, including healing and the truth about His kingdom.

However, for the towns that turned disciples away, their refusal to welcome brought condemnation. Jesus said, "Even the dust of your town we wipe from our feet as a warning to you." Then the disciples were told to tell the residents that the kingdom of God had come near.

The kingdom of God *did* come near—in all towns, it came right along with the gospel message. Residents had an opportunity to welcome the truth and welcome the feet that were carrying good news, but they also were free to turn it away. Those who welcomed the truth about Jesus received favor and blessing. Those who shunned Christ received warning, distance, and judgment. Even the dust of the unwelcoming, unreceptive towns would be wiped off in a strong statement against them.

Just as you can welcome guests into your home in a friendly and kind way or a distracted, rude way, you also have an opportunity to welcome Jesus.

Before you make a quick decision, think things over. What would it mean to welcome Jesus into your home and your life? What would it mean to turn Him away? Consider your preference, and then get ready to open the door. He stands at your door and knocks!

*Lord Jesus, here You are! You stand at the door and knock. I hear Your voice. Today I can choose whether or not I open the door to You. If I do, You will come in, bringing blessing after blessing that I don't deserve. You'll shower me with Your favor and blessing. And if I don't, there are consequences. As You taught Your disciples, there will be warning, distance, and judgment. I'm so grateful for Your willingness to welcome me into Your family once I choose to welcome You into my heart. In Your name I pray, amen.*

## Think It Over

- How can you show kindness to someone you've never met? How could this choice to act kindly make a good first impression?
- If you're prone to creating bad first impressions, what could you work on to change that?
- How do you need to mentally prepare to welcome guests on a moment's notice? How do you need to physically prepare?
- As Jesus says in Revelation 3:20, He stands at the door and knocks. He's ready to come in. Do you hear His voice? Will you open the door? Are you ready to welcome Him?

## Put It into Practice

- While it might feel a little silly, look at yourself in a mirror. Practice smiling at yourself. Try to see what someone else's first impression of you might be.
- Take time right now to choose your response to Jesus. Do you choose to welcome Him? Or do you choose to turn Him away? Take a moment to pray and tell Him about your decision.

## Home Work

Your front door reveals a lot about your home and your personality. Each front door is different; some of the differences depend on whether you rent or own your home, where you live, and what your budget is. To make your front door look its best, take time to wipe it down. Clean off the handle and the threshold. If your door has windows, clean those. If you can hang a wreath, choose one that reflects the personality of your home and your personal style. If you enjoy changing wreaths, update yours with the seasons. Otherwise, choose a tastefully timeless wreath that can be left up for a while.

WELCOME

# *Greeting Others with Your Welcome*

*When he arrived in Galilee, the Galileans welcomed him. They had seen all that he had done in Jerusalem at the Passover Festival, for they also had been there.*

John 4:45

Imagine living during the same time Jesus was here on earth. Imagine hearing all the news about this mysterious miracle maker—news which would have traveled by word of mouth from village to village. Would you travel to catch a glimpse of this man or listen to His teaching? Would you take a sick loved one to beg for His healing?

In Galilee, Jesus' reputation preceded Him. People had heard what Jesus had done in Jerusalem during the Passover; now here He was, entering their region. He walked the streets of their communities and talked to men and women, young and old. And the Galileans welcomed Him.

Their welcome communicated so much. They were ready and willing to get to know this man. They were receptive to hearing and learning from Him. They wanted Him to spend time with them in their community.

Their warm welcome made all the difference. In Galilee, Jesus called many of His disciples. He performed many miracles, including His first public miracle of turning water into wine. And as Matthew 4:23 details, "Jesus went throughout Galilee, teaching in their synagogues, proclaiming the good news of the kingdom, and healing every disease and sickness among the people." Later, the resurrected Jesus promised to see His followers in Galilee where he gave the Great Commission, not Jerusalem (Matt. 28:10, 16–20). Because of their gracious welcome, Galileans were able to reap the benefits of having the Son of God perform much of His earthly ministry right in their midst.

Although the Galileans wouldn't have had any clue about the impact that Jesus would create in their midst or even who He truly was, all of His teaching and healing in their community began with their welcome.

What might happen in your life when you welcome others? Even though Jesus won't walk the streets of your community, you never know what long-term blessings might come as a result of welcoming people. You might not fully understand or realize who you're welcoming at the time, if ever. What might seem like a quick, last-minute invitation could make an unexpectedly lasting difference in the life of you or your guest. And the conversations that you share around your table might blossom into decisions that hold an eternal impact.

The Lord works in mysterious yet mighty ways. You may never be absolutely sure what His good and perfect plan is, but you can still step out in faith, love, and obedience and create a meaningful welcome to people you know well and others you're just getting to know. You can host others and trust the Lord to work through your hospitality. Simply obey by making the invitation and opening your home. Follow through with a prayerful and intentional gathering. Then watch the ways God will surprise you through the way you welcome others.

*Father God, thank You for including examples of hospitality and welcome in Your Word. Sometimes I need to hear how people could and should welcome You, as well as other visitors. Like the Galileans, I want to welcome Jesus into my midst. To reflect my respect for Him, I want to invite and welcome His followers as well. Use me as Your representative here in my corner of the world. Help me welcome people in Your name. Please show me who needs my hospitality. Please stretch my resources, whether it's time or finances or space, so that I can gladly welcome others into my home. Thank You for the opportunity to welcome others in Your name. Amen.*

## Think It Over

- In what ways have you watched the Lord work in your life through the way people have welcomed you into their lives, their circles of friends, and their homes?
- Who is one surprising person in your life? In what ways has he or she surprised you by saying or doing something? How has this person blossomed into someone so much more than you ever expected?
- How have you welcomed the Lord into your life?

- Who would you like to welcome into your home?
- How much do you include prayer in your hospitality efforts? Do you pray about who you should or shouldn't invite to your home? Do you pray over the conversations before your guests arrive?

## *Put It into Practice*

- Before you make any invitations, pray over people you'd like to welcome to your home. Get into the practice of praying first, then inviting.
- Just as the Galileans welcomed Jesus near the beginning of His ministry, it's time for you to welcome someone in ministry too. Who will you invite to your home?

## *Home Work*

What do guests see when they walk in your front door? Some homes are graced with large entryways and foyers that give guests room to take off their coats and stay a while. Other front doors open right into the middle of all the action. Take a moment to consider what your guests see. Try walking through your front door with fresh eyes and think of ways to improve the experience for your guests. Make changes if possible. And if you're dealing with constraints in time, money, or space, don't sweat it. Your hospitality speaks much louder than the impression your guests experience when they walk through your door.

# *Are You Receptive to Welcoming Others?*

*He charged them to take nothing for their journey except a staff—no bread, no bag, no money in their belts—but to wear sandals and not put on two tunics. And he said to them, "Whenever you enter a house, stay there until you depart from there. And if any place will not receive you and they will not listen to you, when you leave, shake off the dust that is on your feet as a testimony against them."*

Mark 6:8–11 ESV

Think about a time when you visited someone and felt completely welcomed. You *knew* you were valued. You knew you found a place where you fit in and belonged.

Now think of a time when you felt anything *but* welcomed. Did you want to bolt for the door and get out as quickly as possible?

Hosts have the ability to make their guests feel welcomed or unwelcomed. They're given a huge responsibility to set the stage for a visit. They also have the unique opportunity to communicate their care and concern while building others up.

When Jesus went from village to village to teach, He sent out His disciples two by two to preach and heal. As they went out, the disciples were instructed to not take anything with them and to stay with strangers. Their potential hosts might welcome them, or they might refuse the unexpected visitors.

If a potential host wasn't receptive to the idea of guests or to the message the disciples were preaching, the disciples now had a testimony, or evidence, against them.

Just like people had the opportunity and choice to welcome or refuse Jesus' disciples and their unexpected requests, you also have opportunities to welcome or refuse potential guests.

Before you're faced with a hospitality decision, what is your overall receptiveness toward guests? Are you typically willing to open your home to others? Or do you prefer to stick to yourself and keep others away? Do you tend to open your doors and sit on your porch, or do you keep all your doors and blinds shut tight while you stay inside your home?

Recognizing your tendency right now and deciding if you'd like to change is a powerful starting point. For example, if you know you'd like to improve your hospitality, determine to make a change. Then start making your home more welcoming, whether it's with furnishings or food or cleanliness.

If you're in the habit of hosting others and you're already comfortable with what you're doing, that's wonderful. Continue with what works best for you. Keep inviting and welcoming others.

If you've completely shut out the idea and practice of hospitality, think about why you've made this decision. What led you to this choice? Have you talked to God about it? Try praying for guidance and see what happens. Will He change your heart or mind?

No matter what stage of readiness or willingness you find yourself in, keep looking for opportunities to welcome others into your home. When you spy an opportunity, follow through. Do it! Receive your guests and show them the love of Christ with your warm welcome.

*Father, I admit that it doesn't always feel easy or even comfortable to welcome guests. I want to change though. Sometimes I feel uncomfortable meeting new people. Small talk doesn't always work out the way I imagine it should. Relationships take unexpected turns. Sometimes I'm more comfortable just sticking to myself. But I want hospitality to become a gift I willingly give to others. I know it's important to You, and I want it to become important to me. Please help me get past my resistance and be willing to invest in the lives of my guests. Even if I'm busy with life, help me set aside time for relationships, especially as You direct people to my home. In Jesus' name I ask this, amen.*

## Think It Over

- When have you felt most welcomed? How did your hosts' kindness stand as a testimony in support of their character?
- When have you felt unwelcome in a place? How did your hosts' rudeness stand as a testimony against them?

- If your willingness or unwillingness to welcome others stands as a testimony, either for you or against you, are you content with the testimony your hospitality offers? If not, what needs to change?
- Do you tend to be receptive to the idea of company and guests? Or do you typically turn away from opportunities?
- What can you do now to prepare for unexpected guests in the future?
- How can you make guests feel welcome in your home?

## *Put It into Practice*

- Practice your receptivity to guests. Welcome others into your home. As you offer a place to sit or something to eat or drink, slow down. Ask your guests thoughtful questions. Listen to what they have to say, without worrying about all the things you can or should do.

## *Home Work*

Where can your guests hang their coats or leave their shoes or purses when they enter your home? Take time to freshen this area up and transform it into a space that truly welcomes others. Whether it involves taking other coats off of your coatrack, cleaning up your mudroom, or straightening up your coat closet, make the effort. Do the work. If you don't have a designated space for welcoming guests into your home, now's a good time to consider where your guests feel welcomed to come in to stay awhile.

# What a Warm Welcome!

*At that time Mary got ready and hurried to a town in the hill country of Judea, where she entered Zechariah's home and greeted Elizabeth. When Elizabeth heard Mary's greeting, the baby leaped in her womb, and Elizabeth was filled with the Holy Spirit. In a loud voice she exclaimed: "Blessed are you among women, and blessed is the child you will bear! But why am I so favored, that the mother of my Lord should come to me? As soon as the sound of your greeting reached my ears, the baby in my womb leaped for joy. Blessed is she who has believed that the Lord would fulfill his promises to her!"*

LUKE 1:39–45

Imagine what Mary must have been thinking and feeling after she was visited by the angel Gabriel. The visit had been a surprise, and even if Gabriel told her that she was highly favored and that the Lord was with her, that praise must have paled in comparison to the news that she, a virgin, would become the mother of the Son of the Most High.

Mary believed Gabriel and was a willing servant, even if she didn't understand all the impossible details. Miraculously, everything happened as Gabriel promised and proclaimed. Pure Mary discovered that she was, in fact, pregnant. She would try to remember everything Gabriel told her and ponder the news that she would give birth to a son and name Him Jesus.

At some point after Gabriel's news, Mary decided to leave her family's home and travel to Judea to see her cousin Elizabeth, who also was experiencing a miraculous pregnancy. Mary could take comfort and relate to this older member of her family who, most assuredly, would understand the miracle and wonder of an unplanned, unprecedented pregnancy.

Mary, who somehow made the sixty- to ninety-mile journey from Nazareth to Judea, would have been tired, especially as a pregnant mama. But she hurried, arrived at the home of Elizabeth and Zechariah, and greeted Elizabeth.

Elizabeth didn't even need to see Mary to know what happened. The baby in her womb, John, leapt for joy. And Elizabeth responded with a welcome that would encourage and bless the weariest of travelers.

"Blessed are you among women, and blessed is the child you will bear!" Elizabeth cried out. Can you imagine what those words would have done for Mary? Here she was, unmarried and pregnant, carrying the Son of God. Most likely, other people didn't believe her. But her cousin didn't have to wait for the news. She knew. Mary was pregnant with the Messiah. All of the waiting was over: God was keeping His promises, and Elizabeth celebrated before she heard any details from Mary.

How did Elizabeth's greeting end? "Blessed is she who has believed that the Lord would fulfill his promises to her!" Blessings. Praise. Belief in the Lord's miraculous ways.

Elizabeth was the hostess to reassure Mary and encourage her with love. While Mary wouldn't always be warmly welcomed by others, Elizabeth honored her and flooded her heart with joy, relief, and confirmation.

Like Elizabeth, you can speak life and hope into the hearts and minds of your guests. You may not have a Holy Spirit-filled baby leaping in your womb to reveal secrets about your guests, but you do have an opportunity to find out what your company might be facing. Do they appear worried or weary? Excited? At peace? Take time to discern how they're feeling and be sure to ask sensitive but thoughtful questions.

While catching up is important, so is the way you impart a blessing. Do your guests feel welcomed and seen? Do they feel heard? Do they feel known? Speak God's truth into their lives and their situations. It will be a gift that continues to bless your guests long after they've returned home.

*Father, thank You for the welcoming example that Elizabeth gave. Oh, how I want to spread joy and encourage my guests with her kind of encouragement and hopefulness. Please help me share my faith in You by the way I greet my guests. Please give me words to speak that will affirm and inspire. Help me point to You in the way I respond to others and the words I choose to use. In Jesus' name I pray, amen.*

## *Think It Over*

- What's the warmest welcome you've ever experienced? What's the warmest welcome you've ever given?
- How have previous hosts blessed you by the things they've either said or done for you?
- What are some key phrases you could use to bless a guest who's visiting your home? What life-giving phrases would you like to hear? Use those with your company.
- What welcoming tips or phrases can you borrow from Elizabeth?

## *Put It into Practice*

- The next time you welcome a guest to your home, try your best to give a joy-filled, meaningful greeting. How can you bless your guest by the kind, affirming words you choose?

## *Home Work*

As you get ready for your events and gatherings, consider how you'll create a welcoming mood. What sights and smells would you like your guests to experience when they enter your home? What would you like them to hear? This week, create a playlist as a musical backdrop for your gathering. You could make your musical selections based on your company's taste or on the mood you'd like to create. Enjoy!

## Section Two

# *Caring for Others with Your Welcome*

With so much going on in the world today, how can you begin to make a difference? In a self-centered society, how can people understand that you actually care about them?

The good news is that you don't have to change the entire world. The even-better news is that you can make a difference—sometimes a very big difference—by focusing on your own corner of the world. When you focus on affecting your sphere of influence by welcoming people, not only is it possible to spur on change but it's also very probable.

Welcoming others certainly happens when you open up your home. But if you don't feel like hospitality is your strength yet, you can begin making a difference simply by having a welcoming attitude and personality in everyday life.

When people feel seen, heard, and known, they experience a welcome. When you take time to look someone in the eye and smile, say hello, or stop to listen, you're extending a welcome. This kind of welcome doesn't require anything but slowing down and giving your time and attention.

As you consider this approach and become more welcoming with your words, your body language, and your attitude, watch for people to be drawn to your friendliness. Listen for the ways they'll open up and confide in you simply because you're willing to listen. Be amazed at how God can use your modest attempts to welcome people in major ways.

When you choose to welcome others, you show to them (and yourself) that you care for them. The following devotions will show you how hospitality was used as a way to care for others in the Bible, and you'll identify the clear call to care for others through your welcome.

# Choosing to Motivate Each Other

*Let us think of ways to motivate one another to acts of love and good works. And let us not neglect our meeting together, as some people do, but encourage one another, especially now that the day of his return is drawing near.*

HEBREWS 10:24–25 NLT

Life isn't meant to be lived alone. Just as God noted during creation that it wasn't good for man to be alone (Gen. 2:18), keeping to yourself isn't part of His plan, even for the introverts of the world. It's good to live in community with other people, and it's especially good to live in community with other believers.

Regardless of how you feel about others, it's refreshing to know the Lord didn't intend for people to live in isolation. We don't have to figure out life all by ourselves. Life is richer when lived in community. And this truth comes with some conditions. Solitude, while refreshing, shouldn't be a main focus in life. Even if you're a true introvert at heart, make sure you're spending time with other people. Face-to-face, in-person socialization is good.

Why is it so important to have the influence and company of others? What are some of the benefits of gathering together? Why invite people to your home? The author of Hebrews pointed out a few advantages. First, when you get together with others—particularly fellow believers in Christ—you can think of ways to motivate each other.

But exactly what kind of motivation and ideas do believers need?

- You can bounce ideas off of each other about how to better show Christ's love to those who don't know Him.
- You could brainstorm good works that would bless others or discuss ways to reach out to your community.
- You also might choose to meet as a way to get to know each other and encourage each other in the midst of the storms and uncertainty of life.

Meeting with other believers is a fantastic way to connect authentically. When you're face to face, ideas flow better—you're able to focus on what the other person is saying instead of looking at each other on a screen or trying to pay attention during a call or figuring out the intention behind a text.

When you decide to meet, you'll need to choose a gathering place. This could be a fantastic opportunity for you to open your home or, at the very least, to practice your hospitality skills even if you're out and about. By choosing to welcome others, you can make sure you actually meet together. You don't have to wait for someone else to take the initiative—choose to make it happen on your own.

As you do, one time may not be enough. You might want to continue meeting. If this is the case, establish a rhythm and find the best times and places to meet. You may want to set aside a particular night of the week or the month. Finding whatever works best for you, you could rotate locations or stick to the same spot. The important thing is to prioritize meeting together. As you do, you'll step out of the temptation to stick to yourself and be a loner—and step into a life that includes Christian fellowship.

*Father, thank You for not expecting me to live this Christian life on my own. Thank You for the gift of sisters and brothers in Christ who can help me grow and spur me on to a better life of service to You. Please bring other believers into my life. Show me how I can encourage them. Please guide us and give us ideas for treating others with the love of Christ through our good deeds. Give us ideas so we can serve our communities and circles of influence for You and You alone. In Jesus' name I pray, amen.*

## Think It Over

- How are you currently showing the love of Christ to others? What are some ways you could improve? What would you like to try?
- How often are you motivated to do good works? Do you have merely good intentions and ideas about good works, or do you follow through and turn your intentions into works?
- How often do you meet with other believers? Are you in the habit of meeting regularly? If not, whom could you meet with? When and where could you meet?

- How do your friends, family, and brothers and sisters in Christ motivate you to reach out and love this world for Jesus? How do you try to motivate others to do the same?

## *Put It into Practice*

- Set a date! Think about a believer you'd like to talk with. Look at your calendar to see available dates and times. Contact the other person and figure out what works best for both of your schedules. Make sure you follow through and meet together!

## *Home Work*

Before guests visit your home, consider decluttering any rooms they will see. Take time to declutter rooms where your guests will spend a lot of time. One of the most obvious places is your living room. Especially if you're planning to spend time sitting around and visiting, prioritize decluttering this space. Remove anything that's out of place and straighten up all that you can. Things don't need to look perfect, but tidiness is welcoming. Even if you don't necessarily mind your own clutter, it might distract your guests. By getting it out of the way, you can devote your full attention to each other.

# *Sharing with Others Means Caring for Others*

*We know, dear brothers and sisters, that God loves you and has chosen you to be his own people. For when we brought you the Good News, it was not only with words but also with power, for the Holy Spirit gave you full assurance that what we said was true. And you know of our concern for you from the way we lived when we were with you. So you received the message with joy from the Holy Spirit in spite of the severe suffering it brought you. In this way, you imitated both us and the Lord. We loved you so much that we shared with you not only God's Good News but our own lives, too.*

1 Thessalonians 1:4–6; 2:8 NLT

Take a moment to think about some of the Christ followers you know and love. What makes your friendships special? Because of your close relationships, how do you share your life with these sisters and brothers in Christ?

When Paul, Silas, and Timothy came to the church in Thessalonica, no doubt they felt weary and wounded. As 1 Thessalonians 2:2 details, "You know how badly we had been treated at Philippi just before we came to you and how much we suffered there. Yet our God gave us the courage to declare His Good News to you boldly, in spite of great opposition" (NLT).

Opposition and suffering are never pleasant or easy to endure. When these early missionaries boldly declared the Good News, the Thessalonians responded and believed. Paul affirmed the Thessalonian church at the beginning of his letter, "We think of your faithful work, your loving deeds, and the enduring hope you have because of our Lord Jesus Christ" (1 Thess. 1:3 NLT). After the Holy Spirit gave the Thessalonians full assurance of the truth of the gospel, their lives were changed: Their work was faithful. Their deeds were loving. And their hope in the Lord Jesus Christ endured, even through severe suffering.

As brothers and sisters in the faith, the church in Thessalonica imitated Jesus as well as Paul, Silas, and Timothy. In return, Paul, Silas, and Timothy shared God's Good News, and their own lives.

When true believers find other true believers, so much can be shared. You can share stories of how the Lord faithfully has worked in your lives. You can discuss biblical truths. You can pray with each other and pray *for* each other. You can build each other up in faith even as the world is so quick to tear down. You can even imitate the faith of each other.

One way to experience this life of community and discipleship is to spend time together. Share your life with other believers. Instead of keeping to yourself, live out your faith and Christian life with others. When you're in a place where you don't know other believers, pray for brothers and sisters in Christ to come into your life. And keep praying. Even if it takes years, the *Lord can answer your prayers.*

As you pray for the Lord to bring Christian sisters and brothers into your life, maintain your own spiritual growth. Read the Word. Study it. Memorize Scripture. Pray regularly. Find a church that teaches the Bible. Worship the King of kings. Do all you can to grow spiritually so that when the Lord brings other believers into your life, you'll be like iron, ready to sharpen and to be sharpened.

*Father God, I'm so thankful You haven't left me alone to live out my faith in this world. Thank You for the sweet gift of friendship and fellowship. I pray You will help strengthen the relationships I have with other believers. Help us to sharpen each other and point each other to Jesus. May we hold each other accountable as we face life in this unbelieving world. No matter what challenges we may face because of our faith, may the encouragement and prayers of other believers help us keep living faithfully for You. In Jesus' name I ask all of this, amen.*

## Think It Over

- Who are some of your sisters and brothers in Christ who have influenced your faith the most? How have you changed since meeting them? How have you thanked them for their impact in your life?
- Currently, who are some of your closest friends who believe in Christ?

- How often do you pray for your friends? How often do you pray for *believing* friends?
- Think through your current spheres of influence. While it's good to reach out to unbelievers, it's also good to have the fellowship of believers. How often do you spend time with sisters and brothers in Christ?

## *Put It into Practice*

- Pray for your current and future Christian friends. Encourage your current friends today with a handwritten note. Be sure to tell them how much you value your relationship and their influence in your life.

## *Home Work*

If you'd like to make your home company-ready, focus on the cleanliness of surfaces in your living room this week. Dust all that you can, from hard surfaces like coffee tables or end tables, to the corners and trim of your ceilings, crown molding, and baseboards. Dust window wells, bookshelves, cold-air return vents, and furnace registers or radiators. If you have the time, go all out and dust lampshades, light bulbs, mirrors, and picture frames. Once you're done with all of the dusting, wash any windows in your living room. You may not get to clean this thoroughly very often, so take a moment to enjoy the finished product.

# A Deep and Sincere Love

*Now that you have purified yourselves by obeying the truth so that you have sincere love for each other, love one another deeply, from the heart. Above all, love each other deeply, because love covers over a multitude of sins. Offer hospitality to one another without grumbling.*

1 PETER 1:22; 4:8–9

In all of your thoughts about hospitality, have you ever considered that welcoming and hosting others is a very practical way to reflect your love? It may not always be the easiest or most convenient way to reflect your love, but it's powerful. Opening your home and welcoming others is a lot like a big mirror that reflects your sincere love for other people and for Jesus.

Throughout his letter to the early church dispersed throughout Turkey, Peter mentioned the need to love. He explained that brothers and sisters in Christ should show sincere love to each other, and he encouraged them to love deeply with all their hearts. He later taught them to love each other as brothers and sisters, and to continue to show deep love for each other. Why? Because Peter knew firsthand that love covers a multitude of sins.

Peter was convinced of this need to love. Because he experienced Christ and His teaching, he knew Christ's commands to love each other. He personally witnessed Christ's perfect example and sacrificial love. After Peter denied Jesus three times and Jesus rose from the dead, the resurrected Jesus asked Peter three times, "Do you love me?" (John 21:15–17). Of course Peter did. His heart was repentant and full of love, and he received forgiveness. If anyone knew that love covered a multitude of sins, it was Peter.

To be more like his Savior, Peter knew he needed to love—and he knew that those who shared a faith in Christ also needed to love.

This deep, sincere love was important, and it didn't involve loving others in word only. Merely saying that you love wasn't enough. Peter intended for believers to love through deeds. And how did Peter suggest loving deeply? By cheerfully sharing one's home with others.

You're welcome to share your home with anyone—that's certainly one way to show sincere love to your brothers and sisters in Christ. But Peter also specifies the importance of sharing your home *cheerfully*, without grumbling or complaining.

What does that kind of cheerful hospitality include? It might involve inviting someone in for coffee or a meal. It might include hosting overnight guests, whether short-term or long-term. As you love others deeply, you'll know what kind of hospitality you can offer, and you'll also realize what kind of hospitality is needed.

Perhaps what's most striking about Peter's request is not just the necessity to love others through hospitality, but the need for love to be at the heart of your hospitality. Do you invite others out of a feeling of obligation? Do you dread welcoming others? Do you feel like you need to host someone just because she hosted you? Or do you get excited about the idea of having someone over? Do you think of what you can do or what you can offer as a way to love your guests well?

As humbling as it may seem to consider that attitude is everything, it's also freeing to know that your relationships and your worth don't revolve around the complexity of your hospitality. You may live in a simple home or offer simple meals, but if you do it with cheerfulness and thoughtful, loving intention, it's better than the fanciest dinner party thrown by a mean-spirited, cold-hearted grouch. Examine your motives. Stop to consider your own emotional temperature. Make adjustments to your moody thermostat and then invite someone over. It's time to show your love through your thoughtful hospitality!

*Father God, it's really wonderful that You sent Jesus to earth on a rescue mission and that His trademark was love. Out of Your own sacrificial love You gave Your only Son. And out of His own love, Christ willingly sacrificed His life. I want Your call to love others to direct my life. You're not calling me to sacrifice everything—just to love. And You're asking me to love well. I pray that I will love deeply. Please create a sincerity in my love for others, so that I don't feel the need to fake it. I want to be genuine in my love, following Your beautiful, genuine example. In Jesus' name I ask this, amen.*

## *Think It Over*

- When you welcome someone to your home, do you cheerfully look forward to your time together? Or does it put you in a bad mood?
- What could you do to create more genuine anticipation or excitement about hosting others?
- How have other people loved you deeply? How has someone shown you sincere love?
- How have you loved others deeply? What are some meaningful things you've done to show that you care?

## *Put It into Practice*

- In his letters, Peter was very direct in his instructions. Followers of Christ need to love each other deeply and offer hospitality to one another. Now that you've clearly heard the call from Peter, it's time to consider how you can put both commands into practice! What's the first thing you will do?

## *Home Work*

Take time to thoroughly clean your living room floor. Depending on what's covering your floor (and the condition of your floor), you may need to use a vacuum cleaner, wet mop, dust mop, or carpet cleaner. Whatever you need to do, clean thoroughly. Before you start cleaning, make sure the baseboards are dusted and wiped clean, then tackle the actual floor. Move furniture out of the way so you can get to often-neglected spots. And if you're feeling really ambitious, wipe down or vacuum your living room furniture.

Devotion 9

# *Never Left on Your Own*

*He came and preached peace to you who were far away and peace to those who were near. For through him we both have access to the Father by one Spirit. Consequently, you are no longer foreigners and strangers, but fellow citizens with God's people and also members of his household, built on the foundation of the apostles and prophets, with Christ Jesus himself as the chief cornerstone. In him the whole building is joined together and rises to become a holy temple in the Lord. And in him you too are being built together to become a dwelling in which God lives by his Spirit.*

Ephesians 2:17–22

Feeling like you fit in and truly belong either somewhere or with certain people is a wonderfully powerful blessing. For believers in Christ, all the awkwardness of feeling like you're an outsider is gone. Jesus bridges any gap. He welcomes you into His family and you're no longer a stranger. You're not a sojourner or foreigner. You belong.

In this amazing reality of the family of Christ, where you're being knit and built together with other believers, Christ is the cornerstone of the household. The entire building of believers of Christ is joined together. No one is singled out and left alone. Not only are you joined together with other believers but you're also being built together in Christ.

Let this truth sink in for a moment. You're not alone. As Hebrews 13:5 promises, Jesus will never leave nor forsake you. You're never left on your own. Not only does the Holy Spirit make His dwelling with you, a believer but He also gives you access to the Father.

Aside from having unconditional access to the Lord of the universe, believers have each other. You're part of the family of God with your brothers and sisters in Christ. You're family here while you live on earth, and you're family for all eternity.

What does this truth of belonging mean for right now? If you know that through the Lord you have unity with other sisters and brothers in Christ, you don't have to wait until heaven to begin spending time together. Just as families spend time together, whether it's talking, eating, celebrating, supporting, or sharing life, you can do that with other believers too. You don't need to wait until your local church plans a gathering—take the initiative to get to know other believers. Spend time together. Get together at your church, in your homes, and in public places. Meet for coffee or a meal, for prayer or a walk. Find a mutual hobby or try a brand-new activity. What you try isn't nearly as important as simply spending time together. Invest in your relationships, because they're a perfect opportunity to build unity in the body of Christ.

As you spend more time with believers and get to know each other, pray for each other. Hold each other accountable. Bear one another's burdens. Encourage in word and in deed. Share what you have. Be the kind of sibling you wish you had and be sure to follow the Holy Spirit's leading. When you feel led to reach out in some way, follow through in obedience.

By following the Lord's perfect plan in investing in relationships with other believers, you won't be left on your own. You can share the adventure of this life with other believers and glorify the Lord as you do.

*Father, from the beginning of time You have known that it's not good for people to be alone. Thank You for establishing a family of believers. I've been hurt by others in the past, and I pray You'll heal my heart. Please give me courage to try again. Please bring dear people into my life who love You and also care about me. I pray I will be able to be a good friend who reflects Christ and loves generously. Please help me experience what You've intended the body of Christ to be like. In Your Son's name I pray, amen.*

## Think It Over

- How often do you feel like an outsider or a loner? How often do you feel connected and part of the body of Christ?
- Which fellow believers do you want to know better? What are some ways you could initiate spending time together?
- Because you're being built up in unity in Christ, what could you do to spend more time with believers?

## *Put It into Practice*

- It's time to invest in your relationships with other believers. Decide whom you'd like to get to know better and then extend an invitation. You may invite your fellow believer over to your home, or you may choose to go out for coffee or a meal. Whatever you decide, set a time and make sure it happens. Enjoy your conversations!

## *Home Work*

Now that you've done all the tedious deep-cleaning projects around your living room, it's time to have some fun! Focus on making your living room both cozy and inviting. Add some comfortable pillows to your couch. (If you already have some, fluff them!) Make sure you have a throw blanket handy in case you or your guest gets chilly. And look around at the accessories or art in your living room. Does it reflect your personality, or is it fairly generic? Take time to add splashes of you into the room, from framing some of your well-loved photos to displaying accessories that make you smile.

# *Welcoming Strangers and Outsiders*

It can feel really comfortable to spend time with your friends. It might feel even more comfortable to spend time with your family. However, as comfortable as all that togetherness feels with people you know best, it can feel *uncomfortable* to start and continue conversations with strangers. Even if you can think of some really thought-provoking questions, what happens when the conversation dries up? What happens when you discover you have absolutely nothing in common or you can't think of any additional things to talk about?

Meeting strangers can feel awkward, but the good news is that meeting new people doesn't have to be something you dread. There's always a possibility that you might get to know someone amazing. After all, didn't you meet all your friends at some point in your life?

Whether you think meeting new people is thrilling or terrifying, everyone needs to meet new people. And when you seek out strangers and outsiders to welcome into your life or your home, you can prepare yourself for some interesting stories and experiences.

It can be really difficult for a person to be new—whether she just moved to the area, decided to try a new hobby, joined a new group, or stepped out in courage and is attempting to make new friends. When a person needs to be welcomed, extend the same kindness you'd appreciate. Warmly welcome strangers.

The Bible is filled with examples of men and women who either needed the kind hospitality of strangers or were gracious enough to welcome others into their homes.

As you welcome new people into your circles of influence, remember that you're living out biblical commands to love others and to practice hospitality. Your obedience to the Word trumps any of your feelings, whether good or bad. Enjoy the welcoming process!

# *The Importance of Welcoming Outsiders*

*When a foreigner resides among you in your land, do not mistreat them.*
*The foreigner residing among you must be treated as your native-born.*
*Love them as yourself, for you were foreigners in Egypt. I am the* LORD *your God.*

LEVITICUS 19:33–34

Which words make you feel welcome? Have you felt welcomed, either by strangers or acquaintances, in any memorable ways?

A warm welcome can go a long way in making a visitor feel a connection. That kind of connection created by kindness is important because it illustrates something Jesus taught. When a Pharisee asked Jesus what the greatest commandment was, He replied, "'Love the Lord your God with all your heart and with all your soul and with all your mind.' This is the first and greatest commandment. And the second is like it: 'Love your neighbor as yourself.' All the Law and the Prophets hang on these two commandments" (Matt. 22:37–40).

For the Israelites, the expectation to love your neighbor as yourself went all the way back to the Jewish law found in Leviticus 19:18, where God commanded, "Do not seek revenge or bear a grudge against anyone among your people, but love your neighbor as yourself. I am the LORD."

Just a few verses later, this command to love others expanded to include foreigners. In fact, Israelites were commanded to love foreigners as themselves.

This idea of loving foreigners as yourself can be viewed as the ultimate hospitality. When you encounter people who are outsiders or new to your community, welcome them. Treat them in a loving, thoughtful way, the way you want others to treat you. The Lord commands that outsiders should be treated just like those who are native-born.

Showing respect to all people, regardless of their nationality or background, is a powerful way to honor the fact that all humans have been made in the image of God. And welcoming all people, regardless of their nationality or background, is a powerful way to show Christ's unconditional love in action.

Welcoming foreigners with kindness and love pleases the Lord as an act of obedience. It can be done in word, by the way you choose to speak to others and the words you use. But it also can be achieved through actions. What are specific ways you can welcome new people to your neighborhood? How can you get involved in welcoming outsiders and visitors to your community?

As you think of things you could do to reach out to others, consider what makes *you* feel welcome. How could you mirror these same acts as a way to greet others and make them feel like they belong? What thoughtful act of kindness would make your day?

Since imitation truly can be a sincere form of flattery, think about how other people have included you and made you feel welcome. Is there anything that was said or done that you can replicate? You don't have to be concerned about brainstorming something completely new. Rather, make the situation easier on yourself and follow other people's ideas and advice. You already know what has made you feel welcome. Don't be afraid to use the good ideas.

As you try to welcome others with the love of Christ, you'll watch your world and your kindness expand.

*Father God, it's a beautiful thing to know that You desire everyone to be welcomed. You want everyone to be treated fairly and respectfully. You want people to fit in and not to feel isolated or lonely. I want to obey Your commands. I want to love other people well and to welcome them in Your name. Please help me look for opportunities to reach out to others who are new. Show me how I can love them in ways that I would like to be loved and welcomed. Bring strangers into my life who need Jesus. It's in His name I pray, amen.*

## Think It Over

- When you've been the new person in a community, what made you feel welcome? What did people say or do to help you feel at home? How can you replicate this with someone else who is new?
- Think about the times you've welcomed people. What did you say? What did you do? What more could you have done to show the love of Christ?

- Why did God say it was important for the Israelites to welcome foreigners? How could similar reasoning apply to you and your life?
- What are a couple ways you could welcome others?

## *Put It into Practice*

- Now that you've thought about what you could do to welcome others, mentally and physically prepare yourself to do this the next time you meet someone new. Think of the words to say. Plan something thoughtful to do, then watch for whom God will bring into your life.

## *Home Work*

It's often said that the kitchen is the heart of the home. Because of that, it's one of the main places people love to congregate. Before guests spend a lot of time in your kitchen, spend some time cleaning it up! When you have an extra moment, your challenge is to clean the countertops. If your kitchen reflects a minimalistic approach, you don't have much on your kitchen surfaces and you'll need only a little scrubbing and deep cleaning. If your kitchen counters act more like clutter magnets, you'll need to spend more time culling through what's on your kitchen surfaces. Don't be afraid to be ruthless! Put away appliances that are rarely used, sort through papers, and put everything away in its proper place. If you have too much in your kitchen, make sure that everything there is something you need to use or something you love. Everything else can find a home somewhere else!

# *Offering Rest and Refreshment to Others*

*The LORD appeared to Abraham near the great trees of Mamre while he was sitting at the entrance to his tent in the heat of the day. Abraham looked up and saw three men standing nearby. When he saw them, he hurried from the entrance of his tent to meet them and bowed low to the ground. He said, "If I have found favor in your eyes, my lord, do not pass your servant by. Let a little water be brought, and then you may all wash your feet and rest under this tree. Let me get you something to eat, so you can be refreshed and then go on your way—now that you have come to your servant." "Very well," they answered, "do as you say."*

GENESIS 18:1–5

What's your typical reaction when people unexpectedly drop by your home? Are you happy to see them? Curious as to why they stopped by? Embarrassed by the state of your home? Annoyed that they didn't ask before they stopped?

The book of Genesis recounts a time when, during the heat of the day, three unexpected guests arrived at Abraham's home. Abraham's greeting and offer revealed much about his heart for hospitality. Perhaps Abraham knew who the guests were, but maybe he didn't. Regardless of his familiarity, this centenarian got up from his seat, hurried to his guests, bowed low, welcomed his visitors, and offered them some refreshment.

When the guests accepted Abraham's hospitality, he was able to be a gracious, thoughtful host who offered refreshing water, food, cleanliness, and rest beneath the shade of a tree. By the end of their visit near the great trees of Mamre, these special guests promised Abraham and Sarah the miracle of their late-in-life pregnancy and the unlikely yet impending birth of their son Isaac.

Abraham's welcome is something we can emulate. Sometimes unexpected guests show up at your door. They may be people you know very well, or they might be complete strangers. You might have known your visitors for decades, or you might greet a service technician at your home for the first and only time.

When guests surprise you, it might feel challenging to drop everything and give a warm and welcoming greeting. After all, if you're in the middle of the busyness of your day, an unexpected visit might throw you for a loop.

But if possible, follow Abraham's example. Welcome others with kindness and generosity. When it's appropriate, offer something to drink or eat. If you and your guest have time, invite your visitor to sit down to rest and visit. Note that Abraham probably didn't expect these visitors to stay for a long time. He simply offered a place for them to refresh themselves.

In these moments when you've had absolutely no chance to prepare your mind or your home, you might feel frazzled. Your home may be filled with messes, or your cupboards might be bare with nothing to offer your guests. When this is the case, try to relax. A welcoming attitude will be what's memorable—not what state of cleanliness your home is in or what refreshments you can offer. Simply offer your kindness and a warm welcome.

As you welcome like Abraham did, you never know what unexpected blessings might come as a result of the surprise visit!

*Father, You are a faithful, covenant-keeping God. Just as You kept Your incredible promises to Abraham, You will keep Your incredible promises to me. Thank You for the way You worked in Abraham's life. I'm so glad I can read about Abraham and learn from his successes and shortcomings. I want to become more like him and have an attitude and a heart that are ready and willing to welcome unexpected guests. Please transform my attitude and help me become more welcoming! I ask all this in Jesus' name, amen.*

## Think It Over

- Your attitude takes center stage when you greet and welcome unexpected visitors. Regardless of whether you're inundated with what feels like a million other things to do or you're home with free time, when guests pop in, you'll quickly discover what a surprise drop-by will do for your mood and attitude. You might realize you're truly not in a welcoming frame of mind, and it's reflected in your words and actions. Or, you may surprise yourself and welcome with gladness, even when you need to stop what you're doing and say hello. Take a moment to think about the possibility

of welcoming an unexpected guest. What's your initial reaction?
- When you've shown up at someone else's home unexpectedly, what welcome do you remember receiving? When have you been welcomed with exceptional kindness? When have you felt unwelcome?
- Would you like to trust the Lord to help you become more hospitable and kind? Do you need to ask Him to help you have a more welcoming attitude?

## *Put It into Practice*

- What are different ways you could welcome unexpected guests? You may want to practice saying a specific phrase—even something as simple as "Welcome! It's so good to see you!" Or, "Come on in!" Or, you may want to stock up on some refreshing goodies just in case you need to invite guests in. If welcoming spontaneous guests is a challenge for you, create an impromptu welcome kit now by gathering a few non-perishable food items. (If unexpected guests never stop by, you'll be able to enjoy these treats yourself.) If you know you'd feel stressed by welcoming guests to a messy home, what can you do to make at least one room more company-ready? Start practicing your welcome now, so that it becomes second nature when someone actually shows up unannounced at your door.

## *Home Work*

You may think about dusting other rooms in your home, but do you often dust your kitchen? Take some time to clean off surfaces you may not clean very often, from the top of your refrigerator to your range hood and fan. Clean off light fixtures and lights, as well as your kitchen windows. Once you start cleaning, look for other surfaces that often escape your notice. If you have extra time, this could be an opportunity to deep clean other parts of your kitchen, like small countertop appliances and anything decorative. You may be the only one to notice how shiny and clean everything looks after you've finished, but that's okay. You can smile every time you see the results of your diligent work.

# Showing Unusual Kindness to Strangers

*Once safely on shore, we found out that the island was called Malta. The islanders showed us unusual kindness. They built a fire and welcomed us all because it was raining and cold. There was an estate nearby that belonged to Publius, the chief official of the island. He welcomed us to his home and showed us generous hospitality for three days.*

Acts 28:1–2, 7

One of the great, freeing truths about hospitality is that your possibilities are endless. You don't have to invite guests in any particular way to any particular event. You don't need to serve one specific kind of meal—or any meal at all. You don't have to feel confined to a certain time of day or week or month. You don't even need to use your home.

Being hospitable and welcoming others are gifts that can be shared at any time and in any way. It's more about your attitude and intention than any specific practices. The apostle Paul experienced this flexibility and creativity during many of his missionary journeys.

When Paul and his companions were shipwrecked, as described in Acts chapter 27, the ship's crew and passengers made their way to the shore of Malta. Once they were there, Paul and his friends discovered the islanders on Malta didn't have much, but what they did have was exceptional kindness. This unusual kindness wasn't extravagant, but it was heartfelt. The islanders built their unexpected visitors a fire to warm them. Because it was cold and rainy, a blazing fire was an incredibly kind way to welcome people who were cold and wet because of their disaster at sea.

The kindness didn't stop there. Malta's top official, Publius, went an extra step and hosted the unexpected visitors in his own home for three days. Not only did Publius give them a place to stay but he also showed them generous hospitality during their time at his home.

We have so much to learn from the islanders on Malta. Kindness can be as easy as thoughtfully and intentionally trying to make life better for others.

If you see that a stranger needs basic comforts, go out of your way to help. Like the blazing fire started to warm Paul on the beach, your help doesn't have to be fancy. It doesn't have to be extravagant. Truly, anything thoughtful you do will make a difference. Simple gifts like a warm coat, a blanket, or a hot cup of coffee can help keep out the cold on a winter day. Umbrellas or ponchos can help people stay dry. A bottle of water can quench someone's thirst on a hot summer day. Basic acts of human kindness go a long way when you choose to be hospitable to others.

But "unusual kindness" like the citizens of Malta displayed? That's a lot more significant than meeting basic needs in a charitable way. Aside from the physical needs of people you might meet, what else can you do to lavish them with the love of Christ? Could you welcome foster children into your home? Or invite widows to come over for some family time? Could you make sacrifices or generously provide acts of "unusual kindness"? As you search for situations to step into, pray for the Lord's guidance. Ask Him to pair you with people who need you the most.

Generous hospitality, like Publius showed, involves liberally sharing and giving. As we welcome others into our homes, may we remember to honor them by abundantly sharing with our guests.

*Lord God, please open my eyes to people who need help, and then show me how I can help them. I don't want to stay focused on my own little corner of the world. I want to be used by You to help others. Bless me with creative thoughts to meet definite, desperate needs. I want to be Your light in this world. Help me show unusual kindness to people who need it the most. Amen.*

## Think It Over

- What are some easy things you can do to prepare yourself to show hospitality to others? Could you store items in your vehicle to give away to people in need? Could you prepare something in your home or kitchen to keep on hand, with the sole intent of blessing others?
- Do you tend to overlook others in need, or do you gravitate toward them?
- How could you show guests generous hospitality in your home? What could you offer or do to make visitors feel welcome?

## *Put It into Practice*

- If you tend to shy away from others, it's time to ask the Lord to soften your heart and open your eyes. Pray for the Lord to shape you into a kinder, gentler, and more obedient version of yourself.

## *Home Work*

Now that you've spent time cleaning the dirty surfaces of your kitchen, it's time for one more surface: the floor! Deep clean your kitchen floor. You know your floor best—whatever method you use to really scrub it, do that. While you're down on the floor, it's also a good time to clean your kitchen baseboards. Because they're high-traffic areas, kitchen floors are notorious for getting dirty, so don't be too upset if they get dirty again soon. Rather, enjoy the results while you can.

# Do You Know Who You Are Entertaining?

*Keep on loving one another as brothers and sisters. Do not forget to show hospitality to strangers, for by doing so some people have shown hospitality to angels without knowing it.*

Hebrews 13:1–2

Does it make you uncomfortable to talk with people you've never met before? Or are you an outgoing person who loves getting to know someone new? Regardless of your comfort level, everyone needs to meet and talk with strangers. It's simply part of life.

One rather obvious fact about meeting strangers is that you don't know who they really are. After all, you've just met.

You may think you can get a good idea of who they might be by the way they look or things they say or mannerisms they show, but those are initial impressions. You might have heard about someone and think you know the person, but your ideas can mislead you. Until you spend a fair amount of time truly getting to know others, you don't know their preferences or pet peeves. You don't know what makes them happy and what breaks their hearts. You don't know who they've loved or what they've lost. You don't know or understand all they've experienced.

Because of this, it's wise to show kindness, grace, and a bit of caution when you first meet a stranger. Remember that your relationship is a blank slate. It's a good idea to ask questions out of curiosity and compassion, but it's also vital to remember to use some restraint and discernment because you don't know who you're meeting.

In the New Testament book of Hebrews, the author specifies the importance of loving fellow followers of Christ and remembering to show hospitality, particularly to strangers. Why is it so important to welcome strangers? Apparently, people have welcomed and hosted angels without realizing it.

Clearly, you don't and can't know exactly who you're meeting. Getting to know people takes time—often a lot of time. And when you meet someone for the first time, you don't have the luxury of getting to know that person very well—even if the person seems to be an outgoing and fairly transparent oversharer. Indeed, when you show hospitality to strangers, you won't know exactly who you're welcoming. Could you show grace and kindness to someone who ends up being a lot more complex or shallow than he or she seems? Of course.

Because you don't completely know the person you're meeting or welcoming, you have no idea if your conversation is exactly what's needed. If you're walking closely with the Lord, listen to His nudges of what to say. Because the Lord does speak to people through other people, something you say or do in passing may be exactly what the stranger needs at that moment.

You may personally welcome strangers into your home, business, or school often. You may welcome strangers into your church, organization, or ministry too. Every day you may show kindness to strangers in a store or while passing on the street. As you do, remember the fantastic reminder from Hebrews 13:1–2. Make it a point to live with kindness and generosity, because you simply don't know who you're meeting.

You may never find out exactly what your acts of kindness and compassion accomplish in a person's life. And on this side of heaven, you may never know exactly who you're greeting or welcoming, which is all the more reason to welcome, speak, and treat others with much love.

*Father, I want to be more like Jesus. I want to live with His kind of authentic love for others. I want to be kind to strangers just like He was. Please help me get out of my own way and leave my comfortable way of living so I can be kinder and more caring. Help me reach out to strangers to help them know that they matter in this world. Please help me to be friendly and welcoming through what I say and do. I don't want to be selfish, Lord. Please help me to show Your love to others. In Jesus' name I ask this, amen.*

## Think It Over

- Can you recall meeting mysterious strangers in your past? Who have you met in an unusual way—a divine appointment rather than part of every-day life?
- What are some ways you could greet and treat strangers with kindness?
- How could you safely but warmly welcome someone you don't know?

## Put It into Practice

- Be kind to a stranger today. It might be your cashier at a store, your mail carrier, or someone you meet for the first time at church. Don't even think about *hosting* a stranger right now—simply work on being kind and asking thoughtful questions that demonstrate you care. Get to know new people in a friendly way, as best as you can.

## Home Work

If your kitchen surfaces are clean, pat yourself on the back and get ready to move on to other areas, like your kitchen cupboards. This cleaning chore may take a while, but that's okay. Take time to make sure everything in your kitchen is in the proper cupboard ("proper" is completely up to you and your discretion). Throughout your week, clean, sort, and purge what you don't need. And organize. When you're finished, everything in your cupboards will look so nice! If you have a lot of extra time, wipe down the front of your cabinets so that everything is clean.

# *Practicing Hospitality*

Have you ever felt intimidated by the idea of hosting others? Does the thought of welcoming guests into your home fill you with anxiety or dread? Or are you willing and ready to open up your home, no matter what it might look like, so that people have a place to gather?

At some point in history, hospitality morphed into a monstrous idea of perfection and precision. Visions of themed food, party favors, and decor eclipsed the importance of true hospitality. All you really need is to welcome guests with generous kindness.

What does this reality-based hospitality look like? If you're going to become the "hostess with the mostess," make sure you have the most kindness, not an extensive variety of decorations or massive quantities of refreshments.

Instead of aiming to host a perfect get-together right away, or every single time you welcome others to your home, remember that you're *practicing* hospitality. Practicing doesn't include precision and perfection like a four-star, gourmet restaurant or over-the-top theming like a luxury resort. It's your personal, real-life attempt. And it's practice, not perfection.

Why even practice hospitality? You might feel compelled to invite and host others, and that's a good thing. You may want to host out of your love for Christ and others. You could show your gratitude for what people have done for you by inviting them into your home.

As demonstrated in the Bible, hospitality and welcoming others is an ongoing act of service that can be practiced. It may never be perfected, and that's okay. Authentic welcomes work powerfully in the lives of both the host and the guests. Biblically speaking, an enthusiastic, genuine, and kind welcome is encouraged.

When you choose to practice more and more hospitality, you might even become known for the way you welcome others—what a good way to be remembered!

# Your Eagerness to Practice Hospitality

*Don't just pretend to love others. Really love them.*
*Hate what is wrong. Hold tightly to what is good. Love each other*
*with genuine affection, and take delight in honoring each other. Never be lazy,*
*but work hard and serve the Lord enthusiastically. Rejoice in our confident hope.*
*Be patient in trouble, and keep on praying. When God's people are in need,*
*be ready to help them. Always be eager to practice hospitality.*

ROMANS 12:9–13 NLT

Is it easy for you to detect someone's true intentions? Can you tell when someone is being genuinely kind versus being phony? Do you find it easy to be kind to most people? Or do you almost always feel like you need to fake or force a kind, loving response?

Because people are people, human nature, behavior, and typical responses don't change over the centuries. So when Paul needed to address his Roman brothers and sisters in Christ, he mentioned what was necessary: genuine love. Apparently, someone in the early church was being two-faced and only pretending to love others. Yet genuine love is essential, and it includes honoring people, working hard, and serving the Lord. And genuine love is absolutely necessary when practicing hospitality.

Paul's letters to the early churches were filled with imperative commands, and his message to the Romans was no different. Paul's clear instructions helped the early church, and they can help you. His assessment that authenticity and love are necessary factors in much of life, including the way you welcome others, is as timely today as it was at the time of his writing.

If you appreciate using to-do lists to organize your priorities and get things done, Paul's list of instructions can be a welcome relief. You don't need to wonder how to live as a believer in Christ. Rather, you can do a quick check and see if your life accurately reflects your faith.

Are you genuinely loving others and showing affection and honor? Do you hate what is wrong and cling to what is good? Are you enthusiastic about the way you serve the Lord and work hard for Him? Are you rejoicing in the eternal hope and promise you have? Are you patient even when you face trouble? Do you pray and then continue to pray? Are you ready and willing to help the needy, especially your sisters and brothers in Christ? And last, but definitely not least, do you practice hospitality? Are you eager to always practice this?

A bit of relief comes with the thought of *practicing* hospitality. If you're truly practicing, you don't have to wait until you're perfect. Hospitality doesn't mean you need to plan a perfect lineup of activities, prepare a perfect meal, and host guests in a perfect home. Rather, you should just do it. If your life or your home is messy, practice hospitality anyway. If your food choices are less than ideal, go ahead and invite someone. Practicing hospitality means that you can open your home in any season of life or any sort of circumstance. Nothing needs to be perfect. After all, reality is filled with imperfection. Just as piano students improve only through practicing, so will your hospitality. Your early attempts at welcoming people into your home will not seem like a concerto of any sort. Practice anyway. Try things out to see what works and what clearly doesn't.

When you consider hospitality as a way of inviting and investing in people, it turns the idea of hosting others from a display of what you can offer, to an opportunity to provide a warm, welcoming place where your guests feel open to share their thoughts and feelings. As you practice hospitality, keep your intentions focused on your guests. How can you best bless the people in your home? Is it through your thoughtful questions and a listening ear? Is it through kindness and encouragement?

As you focus on others and practice hospitality, you'll find you're fulfilling so many of Paul's imperatives for believers. You are loving others with genuine affection. You're holding tightly to the good while honoring others. Your hard work in hospitality is a great way to serve and honor the Lord. You're ready to help those in need, and, through it all, you can pray and keep on praying. Pray for the details of your hosting experience, pray for your guests, pray for conversations, and pray for the Lord to do a mighty work through your sacrifice and hospitality.

*Father, it's refreshing to know that at the heart of hospitality is a heart for other people. Thank You that I can love others well simply by inviting them into my life and my home. I pray You will help me boldly practice hospitality. If I feel uncomfortable, I want to do it anyway. Please use my welcome as a way to genuinely love and honor others. Use my home and my hospitality as a way to help others, whether they have relational, emotional, or physical needs. Please give me discernment to realize how I can best help them and love them for Your glory. In Jesus' name I ask this, amen.*

## Think It Over

- When you consider Paul's list of imperatives, do any of them surprise you? Reviewing his instructions, what do you do really well? What needs improvement?
- Do you regularly practice hospitality? Are you always eager to do it? What do you think could help you add some eagerness?
- Do you usually focus on the externals of hospitality, like the atmosphere and food, or the internals, like what a guest really needs from you?
- Moving beyond a physical focus of hospitality, how can you minister to your guests' emotional needs? How about what they need spiritually?
- If you feel ready and eager to practice hospitality, how could your welcome be a way to help God's people who are in need?

## Put It into Practice

- It's time to start practicing your hospitality! Begin praying about who might need your welcoming home. Once the Lord brings people to mind, make invitations and start practicing. Remember the old adage that practice makes perfect? You don't need to aim for perfection when you host. Intentionally practice.

## *Home Work*

If you've finished cleaning your kitchen cupboards, now's your opportunity to clean your kitchen drawers. Make sure to get everything out, get rid of what you don't need anymore, wash anything that looks dirty, and put everything back with order and organization. And because almost everyone has one, clean your junk drawer. Try to be relentless in parting with things you don't need anymore.

# Come and Stay at My House

*On the Sabbath we went outside the city gate to the river, where we expected to find a place of prayer. We sat down and began to speak to the women who had gathered there. One of those listening was a woman from the city of Thyatira named Lydia, a dealer in purple cloth. She was a worshiper of God. The Lord opened her heart to respond to Paul's message. When she and the members of her household were baptized, she invited us to her home. "If you consider me a believer in the Lord," she said, "come and stay at my house." And she persuaded us.*

Acts 16:13–15

When you come to know Jesus, everything changes. His love and joy and peace flood your soul—and naturally flow to others. Most likely, this outpouring of Jesus' love to others will compel you to do new things. If you kept to yourself in your life before Christ, you may now want to invest in others. Or if you already had a welcoming personality or enjoyed people, you might have a new purpose in all your hospitality.

Paul met many people on his journeys, but Lydia from Thyatira stood out from the crowd. Not only was she well-known for her trade—a dealer of purple cloth—but she also worshiped God. Apparently in this region, people went out of the city to gather and pray by the river. On this particular Sabbath, Lydia was there with other women. Faithful in prayer and eager to worship God, Lydia had a heart ripe for the truth about Jesus.

When she finally heard the good news about Jesus, she responded right away. The Bible explains that "the Lord opened her heart." And when He did, Lydia responded to Paul's message and chose to be baptized.

Lydia's true colors and unforgettable personality shine in what she did after her confession of faith and baptism: She invited Paul and his group of missionaries to her home. But she didn't merely extend a polite invitation and wait for their answer. She pressed the issue by reasoning with Paul: "If you consider me a believer in the Lord, come and stay at my house."

Of course, Paul considered her a believer in the Lord because he had witnessed her decision to follow Christ with his own eyes. Perhaps they both were still dripping wet after Lydia's baptism. So Paul and his friends stayed at Lydia's home in Thyatira. As Luke phrases it, "She persuaded us."

No doubt, Lydia, a woman who already had a heart for worshiping God, would have rejoiced over discovering the truth of Jesus. And no doubt she used a gift and passion she previously had—her heart for hospitality—to bless the Lord's workers. She used her persuasive personality, kind heart, and the resources of her home in a memorable way.

Like Lydia, you may be so excited about your relationship with Jesus that you want to act on it. You may want to go out of your way to bless the Lord's servants. Or you may want to use your heart for hospitality to welcome others into your home as a way to honor the Lord.

As you're ready to obey, realize that some people might automatically respond with hesitation. It seems like Paul and his companions did. Lydia needed to persuade them; you may need to persuade your guests as well. Whether it's by offering a particular meal or by insisting that you want to host, realize that potential guests might want to avoid inconveniencing you. They may not understand that you feel compelled to welcome them into your home.

If you feel the urge to act, do it! If the Lord opens your heart to do or say something specific or if you choose to extend an invitation to others, don't delay. You have no idea how your persuasion will bless others as you glorify the Lord through your obedience.

*Father God, it's a wonderful thing to know that You open people's hearts to respond to Your message. Please open my heart. Help me be receptive to what You want me to know or do. I want to follow through right away in obedience. Please guide me and help me bless my brothers and sisters in Christ as I do Your good and perfect will. You've created good works in advance for me to do. I pray that I will do them! Change me in whatever way to reflect my decision to follow You. In Jesus' name I pray, amen.*

## *Think It Over*

- Is the Lord opening your heart to respond to a specific message? Is He nudging you to do something in particular? If so, what could it be? Will you obey Him?
- What are some ways your life, choices, and habits have changed because of your decision to believe and follow Christ?
- How do you think your hospitality could reflect your excitement for the Lord? When could you reach out to others in hospitality and purpose?
- Who is the last person you asked to stay at your house? Who will be the next person you ask to stay?

## *Put It into Practice*

- Lydia acted on her faith in Christ with the practical but thoughtful action of inviting others to stay at her home. You can do something similar. It's time to act on your faith. Pray about who you can bless and how you can be a blessing. Then step out in obedience and make an invitation.

## *Home Work*

Because so much of life happens in your kitchen, it can easily and quickly become one of the messiest places in your home. This room needs a little extra tender loving care, so spending time tidying and tending to your kitchen will give it the attention it needs. Work on cleaning your fridge. From tossing out foods that are way past their prime to washing down all the shelves and drawers, make the inside and outside of your refrigerator sparkle! Once your refrigerator is clean, take everything out of your freezer and work quickly, getting rid of things that are freezer-burnt or that you know you'll never use. Wipe out the inside of your freezer with a warm, damp cleaning cloth. After the inside is clean, put everything back in order. Now your company can come over, open your refrigerator or freezer to help out in the kitchen, and you won't cringe at the thought of frozen foods tumbling out.

# *Bringing Peace Through Your Hospitality*

*If it is possible, as far as it depends on you, live at peace with everyone. Do not take revenge, my dear friends, but leave room for God's wrath, for it is written: "It is mine to avenge; I will repay," says the Lord. On the contrary: "If your enemy is hungry, feed him; if he is thirsty, give him something to drink. In doing this, you will heap burning coals on his head." Do not be overcome by evil, but overcome evil with good.*

Romans 12:18–21

When someone opposes you, it's never easy to deal with the dispute, neither in the immediate moment when you're faced with conflict, nor afterward when you're left dealing with your emotions. It requires a difficult but conscious choice to forgive and move on. If opposition and conflict continue to build up and you discover you're dealing with an enemy, it can be extremely difficult to move past those feelings of anger, hurt, or resentment.

The good news is that difficult doesn't mean impossible. As Matthew 19:26 reveals, "Jesus looked at them and said, 'With man this is impossible, but with God all things are possible.'" It's possible to choose to forgive your enemies. It's possible to choose to treat your enemies with kindness.

One unique and unexpected way to move past the hurts, insults, and strife in a difficult relationship is by showing kindness through a welcome. While welcoming someone who opposes you or has wronged you seems like a big ask (or even an impossibility), it's the righteous thing to do. As Paul writes in Romans 12, it's vital for believers to treat enemies with undeserved kindness.

If you're at odds with someone, whether it's because of something you did or didn't do or because of something they did, challenge yourself to treat this person with kindness. Your kindness might be a simple hello. That greeting, as difficult as it may feel, is a first step on your way to living at peace. But as Paul describes, your intentional acts of kindness also might include feeding your enemy. You could offer a cup of cold water to refresh someone, especially when it's not expected.

Another huge step in potentially bridging a relationship gap is to host your enemy. This invitation comes with a disclaimer though: Before you welcome an enemy, it's wise to step back and discern if this kind of hospitality would put you in any physical or psychological danger. If the situation presents itself and seems appropriate, find ways to demonstrate kindness and love. Your invitation could take place outside of your home. Consider inviting your enemy out for coffee as an attempt to bridge the gap between the two of you. Or it might look like something as simple as bumping into each other at the store and asking genuine, kind questions that show you care. Welcoming others, especially your enemies, doesn't mean you need to host a big meal in their honor. You don't have to host anything at all. You could attempt to repair the rift by being welcoming in your attitude, words, and actions.

Your efforts may not be reciprocated, and that's okay. Remember you're serving and obeying the Lord, not your enemy. Out of obedience to your heavenly Father you're trying to restore peace, but you're not responsible for the other person's response. You can't change other people's actions or reactions; you can control only your own.

Being welcoming to those who are at odds with you doesn't mean that you need to open your doors in hospitality. You can welcome others back into your life with a friendly greeting or by asking them basic, kind questions. You can choose to forgive, as Christ commanded, providing a grace-filled welcome.

However you decide to bridge the gap and show kindness, when you attempt to mend fences, you'll honor Christ and live out His commands.

*Father, I'll forever be grateful for Your forgiveness. Thank You for loving me so much, even when I opposed You, that You continued to pursue me. I lived as an enemy of Christ, yet He overcame evil with good and rescued me with His great love. With Jesus as my example, how can I mirror and model Your kind of love and forgiveness to others around me? Please empower me to love this way! I want to live at peace with everyone. In Jesus' name I pray, amen.*

## Think It Over

- Do you live at peace with everyone? If not, what relationship do you need to repair? Instead of taking revenge on an enemy, who can you forgive and show kindness to?
- Who needs a figurative cup of cold water from you?
- Thinking of all your relationships with others, how can you love them well? How can you best show them Jesus' love by the words you say and the things you do?
- How have you tried to overcome evil with good? What happened?

## Put It into Practice

- Think about someone who's at odds with you. Decide the best way to begin mending the fence right now. Once you know whom you need to reach out to and what you need to do, decide when you'd like to do it. Spend a lot of time praying about this and create a plan to make this mending process a reality.

## Home Work

If you're looking for something to clean up in your home, it's a great time to deep clean your oven. Whether your oven has a self-cleaning feature, you prefer cleaning sprays, or you use a safe and natural option like baking soda and vinegar, scrub out the inside of your oven. Don't forget about the racks, light, and window.

# *Showing Gratitude Through Hospitality*

*About midnight Paul and Silas were praying and singing hymns to God, and the other prisoners were listening to them. Suddenly there was such a violent earthquake that the foundations of the prison were shaken. At once all the prison doors flew open, and everyone's chains came loose. The jailer woke up, and when he saw the prison doors open, he drew his sword and was about to kill himself because he thought the prisoners had escaped. But Paul shouted, "Don't harm yourself! We are all here!" The jailer called for lights, rushed in and fell trembling before Paul and Silas. He then brought them out and asked, "Sirs, what must I do to be saved?" They replied, "Believe in the Lord Jesus, and you will be saved—you and your household." Then they spoke the word of the Lord to him and to all the others in his house. At that hour of the night the jailer took them and washed their wounds; then immediately he and all his household were baptized. The jailer brought them into his house and set a meal before them; he was filled with joy because he had come to believe in God—he and his whole household.*

Acts 16:25–34

Imagine the life of a jailer in the first century. Undoubtedly facing less than ideal surroundings like the darkness of a primitive jail and prisoner companions, not much would seem uplifting or even worthwhile in each workday. What kind of change would prisoners like Paul and Silas bring to the dank, despairing atmosphere? The two men brought praying and praise. In a depressing place, these men figuratively brought salt to keep out the rot and light to drive out the darkness.

Paul and Silas's faithful witness made a difference. Prisoners and the jailer alike overheard them throughout their confinement. And when a violent earthquake shook the foundations of the prison, it became obvious that Paul and Silas's testimony had affected the people around them. Even though everyone's chains came loose, all prisoners stayed put. Even when the prison door flew open, they remained in their cells.

At first, the pandemonium almost brought the jailer to suicide. Imagine the reprimand and punishment he would face because of a jailbreak. (Acts 12:18–19 explains the consequences of the time: "In the morning, there was no small commotion among the soldiers as to what had become of Peter. After Herod had a thorough search made for him and did not find him, he cross-examined the guards and ordered that they be executed.")

Yet once the jailer discovered everything that had happened—from the earthquake to discovering that his prisoners hadn't escaped—he spared his own life, fell before Paul and Silas, and asked them what he needed to do to be saved.

In the jailer's mind, there was no question: Everything Paul and Silas had said and sung about the Lord was absolutely true. There also was no question that God had the power to save. Whoever Paul and Silas worshiped and served was the only one who could save.

After Paul and Silas explained the simple truth—believe in the Lord Jesus Christ and you will be saved—the jailer responded. He saw the tenderness of Jesus reflected in the words and attitudes of Paul and Silas. He saw the power of Jesus reflected in the earthquake. And he saw the rescue of Jesus in his own life.

What happened next was profound. After the jailer chose to believe in the Lord Jesus Christ, Paul and Silas followed up by speaking the Word of the Lord and baptizing the jailer and his household. This earthquake in the jail wasn't a solitary incident that only the jailer witnessed. Other people were present. And, like the jailer, these other people were changed.

Once his new faith was embraced, the jailer wanted to show Paul and Silas his appreciation, so he washed their wounds, brought them into his house, and fed them. This hospitality came out of sheer joy. The jailer, in his utter joy of believing in Jesus, couldn't help but show Paul and Silas his appreciation.

How do you thank someone for introducing you to Christ? The jailer's initial response was a welcome and a meal. Like the jailer, what can you do when someone affects your eternity? There's no physical gift that can repay a gift of such magnitude. One excellent way to show your thankfulness is by passing along that gift to someone else. And truly, the jailer wasn't the only one who was saved. His entire household embraced the gift of eternal life through Jesus Christ.

One other way to show your sincere, heartfelt appreciation is to prepare a meal and invite someone into your home. This approach is repeated throughout the Bible, and it's as thoughtful today as it was in the Old and New Testaments.

When someone affects your life in a powerful way—whether it involves introducing you to Christ or helping you grow in your faith—show your gratitude with an invitation. Host a meal to show your appreciation. By taking the time to welcome someone into your home, you can open a window into your reality and demonstrate your genuine appreciation.

*Lord Almighty, You have the power to work in people's lives. Nature is under Your command, and people are shaped by You. Thank You for working Your wonders in people's lives. Instead of letting people fend for themselves, You rescue them through Jesus. You deserve praise and thanks when You work in Your amazing ways. May I be quick to recognize the good things You do and even quicker to thank You. May I be quick to thank others for the way they do Your good work and affect my life. I want gratitude to be a trademark of my life! In Jesus' name I pray, amen.*

## Think It Over

- When you've done something considerable for someone, how did he or she show gratitude?
- If you've experienced a transformation due to someone else's influence in your life, how have you shown thanks?
- Is there someone who is speaking the Lord's truth into your life right now? Is this affecting you in an eternal way? If so, how can you show your sincere appreciation?

## Put It into Practice

- Get your home ready! Get your menu planned! It's time to thank someone who is currently helping you grow in your faith. Think of one of your biggest current influences and extend an invitation. It's time to show your appreciation through the kindness of hospitality.

## *Home Work*

If you host a lot of dinner parties or do a lot of cooking, you might use your stovetop a lot. Now that your oven is clean, give your stovetop some attention. Scrub away any splatters, cooked-on grease, and any other mess on your stovetop until it looks very clean. Enjoy the finished product!

# *Being Known for Your Hospitality*

*Gaius, whose hospitality I and the whole church here enjoy, sends you his greetings.*

Romans 16:23

Imagine being known for your enjoyable hospitality. What kind of a welcome would you need to give so that people would associate thoughts of you with how hospitable you are? How many people would you need to invite to your home to gain a welcoming reputation?

When Paul traveled from city to city telling people about Jesus, he stayed in a lot of places. Some towns were quick stops, and others ended up being longer stays. During his extensive journeys, certain people went out of their way to welcome Paul and his companions. But one person's hospitality stood out. While Paul was in Corinth, one man was known especially for his hospitality: Gaius.

As Paul wrote to the early church in Rome, he didn't explain the details of Gaius's practices, but it's fascinating to wonder what this man did to be known for his hospitality. We don't know if he was wealthy or a man of humble means who simply welcomed people often, but something stood out for Gaius to be known for his enjoyable hospitality. And Gaius didn't reserve his welcome for Paul only; he practiced his hospitality and blessed the entire church in Corinth.

To be clear, the city of Corinth, located in present-day Greece, was a Roman colony, so Gaius wouldn't have necessarily needed to experience life in Rome to rub shoulders with Roman believers. But a couple things are certain: Members of the early Roman church knew Gaius, and Gaius wanted to say hello to them.

Like Gaius, you have the potential to be known for your hospitality. You can welcome and treat guests in such a way that they truly enjoy their time with you. It's wonderfully freeing that we'll never have any idea what food or drink Gaius might have served his guests or what his house looked like. We don't know if he hosted elaborate parties or simple gatherings. We'll never know if he was the life of the party or a man who truly was interested in getting to know his guests by being a good listener and thoughtful host.

This mystery of Gaius is encouraging. As much effort and time you put into preparations for your guests, they will, most likely, forget many of the details. No one may remember exactly how your house was decorated or the food you served. But they will remember the time spent with you and how hospitable you were.

Even though the details of his life and home are a mystery, we can guess that Gaius was consistent and intentional about his efforts. Because he reached out to the entire church, he wasn't trying to be selective in his guest lists. He was trying to be welcoming. And he blessed a whole bunch of people in the process.

Similarly, your consistency and intention are important. People will remember if they enjoy your hospitality. They'll want to come back and spend time in your presence. They'll remember the way you made them feel welcomed and wanted.

Instead of getting tripped up by obsessing over details, change your obsession to a heart for hospitality. Who can you host next? How often do you feel comfortable opening your home? Who needs your hospitality?

As you focus less on logistical details and more on helping people feel the love of God through your hospitality, you will become more and more like Gaius. You'll radically bless others as they appreciate your hospitality.

*Heavenly Father, thank You for the example of Gaius. Thank You for his heart for faithful, enjoyable hospitality. Whatever he did made a difference in the lives of so many. If it would be Your will, Lord, I would like to be more like him. Please help me reach out to brothers and sisters in Christ around me and welcome them in hospitality. Please help me create an enjoyable atmosphere and be a welcoming follower of Christ. Change my corner of the world through my hospitality. In Jesus' name I ask this, amen.*

## *Think It Over*

- Putting aside specific hospitality details, use your imagination for a moment. What might Gaius have done to welcome Paul and the Corinthian church? What made the early church enjoy his hospitality?
- Who comes to mind when you consider enjoyable hospitality? How does this person make you feel welcome? What specific things are done to make you feel at ease?
- How could you be known for your hospitality? What particular hospitality traits or characteristics are your strengths? How could you use these traits to welcome and bless others?
- Realizing that the details of a hosted event don't have a lasting importance, how might you begin to relax and forget about trying to host the "perfect" occasion for guests? How could you change your focus to create an overall atmosphere that people enjoy?
- How can you become more like Gaius and be known for your enjoyable hospitality?

## *Put It into Practice*

- Inspired by the enjoyable hospitality of Gaius, it's time to start reaching out to others! Who can you invite at the spur of the moment? (Remember, it's not about what your home looks like or what kind of food or drinks you serve. It's about your spirit of hospitality.) Extend the invitation!

## *Home Work*

To finish up cleaning your kitchen for company, focus your efforts on your pantry. Your pantry options will differ, depending on what your kitchen is like, but focus on the cupboards and drawers where you store food. Tidy them up, making sure you get rid of food that's past its prime. Wipe down shelves, consolidate what you can, and make it an organized place.

# *Working for Hospitality*

Part of the reason hospitality can seem intimidating to many people is their need for preparation. Instead of opening their doors and welcoming people in, hosts typically focus on planning and preparation. All of those plans and preconceived ideas of what a welcome "should" include have a way of stalling even the most eager host. Typically, when you invite a guest to your home you have some sort of an idea of what you'll serve and do. If you don't, you'll find yourself facing confusion and a lack of clarity.

Preparations don't need to be complex though. Some thoughtful, strategic planning and physical preparations can make the entire event a lot less stressful than hoping everything will turn out or waiting until the last moment to figure everything out.

By planning and preparing for your hospitality efforts, you'll find you're building your home in a very biblical way. Along the way, you may discover that preparations don't solve every problem or make everything easier, but it's okay. With a solid plan in place, you're better equipped to take on all the unexpected hosting challenges.

As you prepare to host and welcome others, prioritize people over things. Even when you have a long to-do list and think you need to accomplish or prepare so much around your home before you open your doors to company, remember to keep your relationships first. The chores and preparations are nice, but not necessary. If you need to decide where to invest your time, energy, and attention, choose people first.

This focus on making a solid plan then diligently following through with preparations is biblical. Work can glorify the Lord. When you do the hard work in your home, you get to reap the benefits along with your guests. Yet for as much hard work as you do, remember to prioritize your guests and relationships.

# *The Necessity of Preparations*

*Then came the day of Unleavened Bread on which the Passover lamb had to be sacrificed. Jesus sent Peter and John, saying, "Go and make preparations for us to eat the Passover." "Where do you want us to prepare for it?" they asked. He replied, "As you enter the city, a man carrying a jar of water will meet you. Follow him to the house that he enters, and say to the owner of the house, 'The Teacher asks: Where is the guest room, where I may eat the Passover with my disciples?' He will show you a large room upstairs, all furnished. Make preparations there." They left and found things just as Jesus had told them. So they prepared the Passover.*

LUKE 22:7–13

For Jews, Passover is one of the most sacred nights of the year. To commemorate this annual celebration of God's faithfulness, many, many preparations need to be made. Thorough cleaning is necessary. Food is prepared a specific way, with specific ingredients. Not only does the preparation take a lot of time but everything must be done in a particular way.

The day before Jesus was betrayed and arrested, He asked Peter and John to prepare for that evening's Passover meal.

While Jesus' disciples would have known how to make preparations, they didn't know where the Passover meal would take place. When they asked Jesus, He gave them specific instructions, telling them how to find the man who would lead them to the place and what they should say to the host.

The disciples did just as Jesus had instructed and found every detail to be just as He described. Once they got to the room, the men busily prepared for the Passover meal that would be served hours later: the Last Supper.

Because the Passover was so familiar to the Jews, the Bible doesn't detail a list of instructions Peter and John would have followed. We have no way of knowing exactly what the disciples did. How did they gather the food? Who did the cleaning? Did they have written instructions and a planned schedule, or was everything committed to memory after preparing the feast year after year? Did they prepare alone, or did their family members help out?

Regardless of what Peter and John did to prepare, we can be certain that a lot of work was necessary. The same is true when you host a feast at your home. (We'll look into this more in Section Eleven.) Perhaps you routinely host a certain holiday meal year after year. Or maybe you share hosting responsibilities with other family members or friends.

If you host a large dinner occasionally, you know that it includes a lot of work. From large grocery shopping trips to days of cleaning, to hours (or even days) of cooking, hosting a feast is exhausting. By the time everyone is seated and all the food is served, you might feel like you'd rather collapse into your chair and nap instead of enjoying all your hard work.

Especially when you host a holiday meal for the first time (or first few times), it can be really tricky to get all the timing worked out so that your entire menu is done at the right time.

And if you routinely host banquets and holiday feasts, the work doesn't disappear. It might seem to get easier because you know what to do. It might go slightly quicker if you can figure out a good routine and remember it from year to year, but it still requires an extensive amount of work.

That's part of what makes a special event special: Much more work and time and effort are needed for a feast or a holiday than for other days throughout the year. If it required the same amount as every other meal on every other day, it wouldn't be a special event.

But because it *is* a special event and because so much attention and work are required, the opportunity creates a time for celebration.

The next holiday or feast you're celebrating and hosting, remember that even if all your hard work is tiring, it's worth it. All of your effort makes a special event that much more special.

*Father, thank You for the gift of preparation. Instead of feeling overwhelmed by all that needs to be done before I open up my home for a feast or celebration, please help me step back and remember what a gift it is to welcome people into my home. Please give me clarity of thought as I make plans for my upcoming dinner. Please help me manage my time well and cook as if Jesus were one of my guests. Help me find joy in working hard for Your glory. In Jesus' name I ask this, amen.*

## Think It Over

- If you want to host a large dinner, planning well ahead of time can make your experience much smoother. To begin, consider what you plan to prepare and clean in your home before guests arrive.
- Other plans of great importance include your menu. What do you plan to serve? Will you ask guests to bring anything? How long does everything take to prepare and cook?
- Once you know what you'll serve, what groceries do you need to buy?
- Closer to the date of your event, start working. Clean. Go shopping. Start preparing food. Set the table or decorate. Figure out specific times when foods need to be cooked.
- Jesus entrusted Passover preparations to two of His closest disciples. The good news for you is that you don't have to do all the work on your own. Who could you ask for help?

## Put It into Practice

- What holiday is coming up next? Will you plan to host a big party or event? If so, start thinking about ideas and plans now. It's never too early to begin the preparations!

## Home Work

Once your kitchen is clean enough for company, spend a while preparing for actual guests. Start gathering and organizing your plates and bowls. Know where you keep everything. Refresh your memory so you can see exactly what you have. Do you need anything for guests? Do you need anything for yourself? Make a list, if needed, then neatly put everything away.

# *Building Your House with Wisdom*

*A wise woman builds her home, but a foolish woman tears it down with her own hands.*

PROVERBS 14:1 NLT

Intention is everything, especially when it comes to where you live. So much can be done to build and maintain and improve your home. But at the same time, so much can tear it down. If you don't intentionally slow down and consider exactly what you're doing (or not doing), you may not realize if you're building your home for the better or actively tearing it down.

As Proverbs 14:1 explains, the entire issue of building up or tearing down your home boils down to wisdom and foolishness. Sometimes it's not easy to determine if what you're doing in your home is wise or foolish. To help discern, consider the actual environment of your home.

First, consider attitudes. No matter if you live alone or if your home is filled with people, do you have a good attitude about who lives in your home? How well do you communicate? If you could imagine yourself as an emotional thermostat, are you pretty chilly? Or warm?

Of course, everyone experiences mood swings, but if the relationships within your home are irritable or argumentative, what can you do to foster a more inviting atmosphere? Prayer has an amazing way of changing hearts and attitudes.

Aside from prayer, perhaps other adjustments can be made to reduce stress or brighten people's days. Anything, from home-baked goodies to a picked-up room or a shared joke, can make a positive difference. All could be wise and helpful ways to build your home.

Apart from the way you build up the emotional strength of your home, what about the actual structure of your home? What are you doing to build and maintain it? What simple aesthetic changes can you make to improve your home? Could adding a few comfortable touches, like updated throw pillows, a cozy blanket, or lamps make a big difference?

Does your home need maintenance work to add to its value and comfort level? Do you need to budget and plan for renovations? Or would something as simple as a thorough deep cleaning or time set aside to purge a mess make a noticeable improvement? By committing to work on these projects and following through, you're wisely building your home and establishing a better place to live.

On the other end of the spectrum, you could tear your house down by neglecting to make improvements, either by choice or neglect. When you ignore disagreements in your home or you let hurts and bad feelings fester, your home begins to crumble. If you neglect to fix something, whether it's a drippy faucet or a major maintenance issue, your home might face catastrophic damage. And if the messes keep piling up due to a lack of time or interest or energy to tend to them, they could grow into something much bigger and more difficult to tame.

By making a daily choice to build up your home, you'll wisely care for what's been entrusted to you. That wisdom will help you establish a more welcoming home, both for yourself and others.

*Father God, I want to be wise. I want to build my home and create a welcoming place filled with encouragement and love. I also want to care for the belongings You've given me. Please help me carve out time to better manage what You've given me, whether it's relationships or space or stuff. And please forgive me for the many times I've torn things down, whether intentionally or unintentionally. Sometimes my words and attitudes and behavior get in the way. Please help me. I want to change! In Jesus' name I pray, amen.*

## Think It Over

- How are you wisely building your home? How are you building your home emotionally? Are you building it spiritually? How are you physically building your home?
- What are some things you do that tear down your home?
- How could you focus better on matters around your home, both big and small? How could you incorporate the art of nurturing to better build your home?

## *Put It into Practice*

- It's time to get building! In the next week, focus on one relationship or attitude to pour yourself into at home. How can your nurturing spirit make a noticeable improvement?
- It's also time to focus on one home improvement project. Which one area of your home can you give your undivided focus? What needs your time and attention? Get working whenever you can, whether it's decluttering a drawer or deep cleaning a countertop. Make sure you make one visual improvement this week.

## *Home Work*

Once your plates and bowls are gathered and organized, focus on your glassware. Gather and assess how many glasses you have, as well as your coffee cups, teacups, and any other container you use to serve beverages. As you gather everything, you might notice mismatched cups or things you'd like to upgrade. Before you neatly put everything away, update your shopping list, if necessary.

# Are You Trying to Do It All?

*As Jesus and his disciples were on their way, he came to a village where a woman named Martha opened her home to him. She had a sister called Mary, who sat at the Lord's feet listening to what he said. But Martha was distracted by all the preparations that had to be made. She came to him and asked, "Lord, don't you care that my sister has left me to do the work by myself? Tell her to help me!" "Martha, Martha," the Lord answered, "you are worried and upset about many things, but few things are needed—or indeed only one. Mary has chosen what is better, and it will not be taken away from her."*

LUKE 10:38–42

"Are you a Martha or are you a Mary?" This question is asked in Christian circles as a way to discern anything from personality types to preferences of organization, cleanliness, or overcommitment.

It all stems from one of the most familiar accounts of hospitality in the Bible, when Jesus is welcomed into the home of Martha. While we don't know many details about Martha, we know that she was a sister to Mary and Lazarus. We also know Martha had a home in Bethany and she willingly opened it to Jesus and His disciples on different occasions.

Welcoming people into your home can entail a lot of work. Martha is known for focusing on all of her busyness, hard work, and preparations. Imagine being invited to Martha's home for a meal—she would make sure you were served the best she could offer.

Even though Martha had an incredible heart for opening her home and hospitality was one of her strengths, she got caught up in all of the details and preparations. Truly, she would have much to keep track of as Jesus and His twelve disciples were dining at her home.

Most likely a realist, Martha knew the work wouldn't get done on its own, so she got busy. She stayed busy. As she worked, trying to get everything ready for Jesus and His disciples, she began to realize something: Her sister wasn't helping.

When Martha went to find Mary, she found her sister sitting at the feet of Jesus, hanging on to His words of truth. And instead of letting Mary sit and enjoy the company of Jesus, Martha began to complain. Perhaps she first started dwelling on negative thoughts about her sister or about all the work that was still necessary. At some point, all of her thoughts took a turn, and she switched from simmering to spewing her frustration to Jesus, who was there as her guest, her friend, and her Lord.

We'll never know if she tried to get Mary to help out earlier, but Martha approached Jesus with a lot of frustration: "Lord, don't you care that my sister has left me to do the work by myself? Tell her to help me!"

Lord, don't you care? Of course Jesus cared, and Martha would have known that. In the comfort of her relationship with Him, she didn't shy away from complaining and frankly telling Him about her stress.

Jesus also was frank with Martha when He corrected her for being worried and upset about many things. Yet her worries and concerns weren't necessary. Only one thing was, and it was there right before her eyes. Amid Martha's busyness, details, and work, she missed the necessary thing: taking time to sit and enjoy Jesus, as Mary was doing.

Jesus said that Mary chose what was better. Jesus is infinitely better than all the work and details that go into a hospitable welcome. He's infinitely better than our to-do lists and all of the work that keeps us busy each day.

While all of the planning and preparation certainly would have made a warm and welcoming gathering, it would have disappeared as quickly as the last dishes were washed and dried. Yet what Mary chose to invest in would not be taken away from her.

As you host, be careful to not get so wrapped up in the details and work that you miss out on what's most important. Slow down and take time to savor your Savior. Don't forget to enjoy and invest in the relationships with the people who are sitting around your table. It will be tempting to get up and keep busy, making sure that everything is just so, but focus on what won't be taken away from you.

*Lord Jesus, thank You for speaking truth into Martha's life and mine. While preparations need to be made, please help me to avoid getting so wrapped up in every detail that I miss out on what's truly important. I don't want to complain about all the work I have to do or a lack of adequate help. Please help me to see my hospitality as a way of serving You. It's a good gift, and I don't want to take it for granted. In Your name I pray, amen.*

## Think It Over

- Is it easier for you to focus on details and preparations like Martha, or would you rather sit back and enjoy people and relationships like Mary?
- If you tend to focus on details, how could you make people a priority in your housework and hospitality?
- What are some practical ways you could build preparation time into your schedule so that you're not so swamped with work once guests arrive?
- How can you intentionally carve out more time to enjoy the people God has brought into your home, either the family that you share your home with, or short-term guests?

## Put It into Practice

- Decide that when you host your next guests you will not spend their entire visit in the kitchen. Figure out a way to make sure all preparations are done ahead of time so you can sit back and enjoy your time with people.

## Home Work

Now is a good time to gather, sort, and organize all of your silverware and serving utensils. Think about how and where you store them. Do you need to make changes? Are any of your utensils rarely used? Or unusable? Don't be afraid to downsize what you don't need but keep what you love and use.

# Preparing a Place for You

*My Father's house has many rooms; if that were not so, would I have told you that I am going there to prepare a place for you? And if I go and prepare a place for you, I will come back and take you to be with me that you also may be where I am.*

John 14:2–3

In what could be one of the most encouraging and exciting statements to believers, Jesus told His disciples about His Father's house. Not only does His Father's house have many rooms but Jesus Himself promised to go there and prepare a place for His disciples. Once the place is prepared, then Jesus will return and take His followers to be with Him.

Which of the two is more exciting for a Christ follower? Knowing that Jesus is preparing a place for you right now? Or that He will come back to take you with Him so that you will be where He is? Both aspects are thrilling.

It's impossible to imagine the preparations Christ is making for us. What could possibly be involved as He prepares a place for you? John 1:2–3 explains, "He was in the beginning with God. All things were made through Him, and without Him was not any thing made that was made" (ESV). God created this world, and His creativity and eye for beauty are astounding. In Him all things hold together. He creates, He establishes, and He knows exactly what is necessary.

Just as mind-boggling as it is to try to fathom what our prepared rooms might be like, it's also amazing to realize that Jesus will come back. The Bible is crystal clear about this. And when Christ does return, He will take those who trust and worship Him to be with Him. You won't be alone anymore. You will be with Jesus where He is.

We could ponder these truths in awe for a while. But while it may seem trivial in comparison, it's also possible to learn a lot about homes and hospitality through Jesus' words. How so?

First, good homes are prepared. Jesus is actively preparing a place for believers. Similarly, if we expect people in our homes, from family to friends or residents to guests, we can spend time lovingly and thoughtfully preparing a place for them.

Why go to the hassle of preparation? When you take time to prepare for others, you show how much you care. You take time to think about someone's preferences and needs.

Second, by preparing, you're not left scrambling at the last moment. Rather, detailed elements are planned, purchased, and prepared. You can spend time with your guests when they arrive, instead of rushing to throw things together.

Jesus wants us to be with Him in a prepared place when we arrive. Likewise, we can spend time enjoying the people in our homes once they arrive. Think of the way He and Mary sat together while Martha was distracted by preparations. Jesus said Mary chose the better thing, which would not be taken away from her: time with her Savior. When you're worshiping the Lord of lords in His Father's house, He won't be busy with distractions. His preparations will be done. He'll be spending time with you.

Keeping this in mind, don't rush off to prepare or work around your house in a last-minute frenzy while your guests are arriving. Be prepared so you can take time to soak in the conversations and enjoy the time together. And remember—just as you get to enjoy these relationships and visits here on earth, one day you'll enjoy an even deeper relationship alongside Jesus forever.

*Lord Jesus, I am so thankful You went ahead to prepare a place for those who love and trust You. I can't imagine what it will be like to be with You in Your Father's house, but I'm so grateful that because of Your sacrifice I'll find out! Thank You for Your preparations. In Your name I pray, amen.*

## Think It Over

- If you believe in Him, Jesus is preparing a place for you right now. What preparations do you think He could be making?
- Jesus is preparing a wonderful place for you, but that will pale in comparison to actually being with Him, the King of kings and Lord of lords. What are you looking forward to the most?
- Here in your earthly home, what preparations could you make to show

your guests that you have their best interests in mind?
- Is it easy or difficult for you to spend time focusing on your guests when they arrive at your home? What could you do to make sure they are your central focus?

## *Put It into Practice*

- Once you have thought about preparations to make before your guests arrive, is there anything you can do now to make your future hosting opportunities easier? Can you do something right now to lighten your load?

## *Home Work*

Your dining room should be fairly well cleaned by now, especially since you've taken an inventory and organized all plates, bowls, glasses, cups, silverware, and utensils. Do you feel ready to invite guests for dinner? The last dining aspect to work on is gathering and organizing your serving platters, serving bowls, and any pitchers. If you use an item to serve food or drink, make sure it's clean, and put it somewhere easy to access when needed.

# Welcoming Your Neighbors

How well do you know your neighbors? So often—perhaps *too* often in many communities—people have no clue who lives around them. Depending on your neighborhood, your comfort level with getting to know strangers, or your concern about anonymity or safety, might leave you content simply walking to your door, entering your home, and then shutting out the rest of the world.

As you bloom in the home where God has planted you, pray for discretion and discernment, but also pray for a willingness to open up and get to know your neighbors. After all, how can you fulfill the biblical command to love your neighbors if you don't even *know* who they are?

As you get to know your neighbors and love them with the love of Christ, you may face noticeable obstacles, like trust issues or the fear of being inconvenienced. Don't shy away from these issues. Pray about them. Pray for guidance and direction, pray for a change of heart, and pray for opportunities to get to know your neighbors.

Depending on your living situation, you may need to pray for new neighbors. For example, if you know you're in a very temporary living situation, pray for the next neighbors you'll have. But also take time to pray for your current neighbors. Even if you don't know them well, and even if they tend to stay indoors all the time, pray for them. The Lord has brought you to your current home at this particular time for a reason. Be a blessing to your neighbors through your prayers and your love for Christ.

As you reach out and get to know your neighbors, know that you're not only fulfilling biblical commands but you're also following the example of many believers in the Bible.

Devotion 23

# *It's All About Love*

*"Teacher, which is the greatest commandment in the Law?" Jesus replied: "'Love the Lord your God with all your heart and with all your soul and with all your mind.' This is the first and greatest commandment. And the second is like it: 'Love your neighbor as yourself.' All the Law and the Prophets hang on these two commandments."*

**Matthew 22:36–40**

When you consider hospitality, what's the first thought that comes to mind? A warm welcome? Food? A clean house? Friends? Family? Conversation?

How about love?

When Jesus was asked about the greatest commandment, love was at the center. He didn't offer an alternative or give a long list of additional requirements. Love was it. Without a doubt, you know that to love God with all that you are and all that you have is the greatest thing to do. The next greatest thing to do is to love your neighbor as yourself.

This reality might be a wake-up call. It's easy to imagine that if you could just *do* more or *be* more, everyone would benefit. But if love isn't your motivation, then you might as well save your time and energy.

Paul wrote, in 1 Corinthians 13:1–3:

> If I could speak all the languages of earth and of angels, but didn't love others, I would only be a noisy gong or a clanging cymbal. If I had the gift of prophecy, and if I understood all of God's secret plans and possessed all knowledge, and if I had such faith that I could move mountains, but didn't love others, I would be nothing. If I gave everything I have to the poor and even sacrificed my body, I could boast about it; but if I didn't love others, I would have gained nothing (NLT).

Since love should be at the heart of a believer's life, all words, thoughts, motives, intentions, and invitations need to flow out of love. Keeping this motivation in mind, our hospitality for others needs to come from a heart of love. We need to extend a loving welcome to our neighbors, the same welcome we'd appreciate. And we need to create this loving experience for others, in response to our love for God.

Welcoming and hosting out of great love may look or feel different than the welcome we typically have in mind. It may be a lot more relaxed than you imagine. Maybe it includes more than you're typically willing to offer. Whether you need to radically change the focus of your hospitality or keep doing exactly what you've done well, your hospitality definitely should focus on others.

No matter what food or drinks you serve (if you serve anything at all) or where you welcome your guests, remember to focus on people instead of everything else. Granted, it's possible to love others very well by planning and serving a beautiful spread of delicious food, but it's not necessary. There's a good chance your guests won't remember what you served or what the surroundings looked or felt like. But they will remember if you ask thoughtful questions, offer encouragement, and welcome them with a loving attitude and words. They'll remember the laughter and togetherness.

Just as Jesus taught that the second-greatest commandment in the Law is to love your neighbor as yourself, you can deduce that the same importance is true in hospitality: Love your guest as yourself. As you do, your love for the Lord your God will bubble over and set the stage for a wonderful visit and hospitality that energizes and encourages others.

*Lord Jesus, during Your time on earth You taught people time and time again about the importance of love. You wanted Your followers to be known by their love for You and love for others. I want to love others well out of obedience to You. Plus, it will add a lot of joy to my life. Please help me do it. While I want to love guests well through thoughtful hospitality, please help me place greater importance on relationships. Help me remember to focus on people more than things. Please bring people into my life and into my home who need Your love. Help me to show it through my actions and words. In Your name I pray, amen.*

## *Think It Over*

- The love you show others through your hospitality reflects your love for and obedience to the Lord. How do you feel about this?
- What is the first thought or idea that comes to your mind when you think about hospitality? Is this based on a biblical principle of hospitality? Or something you've observed in current culture?
- What would your hospitality look like if it centered on loving others?
- Is it easier for you to focus on loving others really well or creating a showplace with beautiful surroundings and delicious meals?

## *Put It into Practice*

- Who needs your listening ear and attention right now? How can you welcome this person and love him or her well? It's time to get started! Reach out and make an invitation.

## *Home Work*

It's time to care for an area of your home that might be overlooked or forgotten. Wherever you eat your meals, whether it's a kitchen or dining room, spend some time caring for your table and chairs. Dust them, polish them, do whatever you need to do to care for them. It's not the most obvious cleaning task, but tables and chairs are used frequently.

# *Living as a Trustworthy Neighbor*

*Don't plot harm against your neighbor, for those who live nearby trust you.*

Proverbs 3:29 NLT

A lot of trust is necessary in everyday life. If you slow down to think about your daily habits and routines, you'll quickly realize you need to trust a lot of people for your survival. When it comes to eating, you trust that your food is grown, manufactured, and prepared safely and correctly. If you're driving down the road or walking across the street, you trust that other drivers will follow traffic laws. You trust that professionals are skilled in what they do (from accountants to electricians, bankers to barbers, and pilots to plumbers) as they perform their jobs in everyday life.

If you consider where you live, even more trust is needed. It's a relief to live in a home that has electricity or appliances you trust to work reliably and safely. It's nice when you can trust that you live in a home that keeps outdoor elements like wind and rain where they should be—safely outdoors. And if you're blessed with good neighbors, it's a huge relief to not live in fear or dread of what's going on next door or what might happen.

While we need to trust that other people are competent or will try to help instead of harm us, it's infinitely more important to put our ultimate trust in the Lord. He is the one who leads and guides. He protects and provides for us in ways we can't observe or comprehend. He orchestrates all things.

As Colossians 1:15–17 explains, "The Son is the image of the invisible God, the firstborn over all creation. For in Him all things were created: things in heaven and on earth, visible and invisible, whether thrones or powers or rulers or authorities; all things have been created through Him and for Him. He is before all things, and in Him all things hold together." In Jesus, all things hold together, including all things in your life and your safety. Because all things hold together in Him, you can trust Him.

Regardless of who your neighbors are and how much they abide by the law, Christ followers can rest in the truth found in Psalm 4:8 (NLT): "In peace

I will lie down and sleep, for you alone, O LORD, will keep me safe." No matter what storms may rage in the world or your neighborhood, it's possible to lie down and sleep because of the Lord's unexplainable peace.

You might be able to sleep more soundly at night if you live in a neighborhood that's relatively safe. While it's never guaranteed, it's a relief to be able to trust your neighbors. And not only is it a gift to have safe, trustworthy neighbors but it's also important to *be* a safe, trustworthy neighbor. Be Christ's ambassador right where you live, always willing to love others through your care, concern, and help.

Proverbs spells out the importance of being a reliable, honorable neighbor. Because people who live nearby probably trust you, it's important that you seek the best for your neighbor. Perhaps Jesus described this best when He said you should love your neighbor as yourself.

Seeking the best for your neighbor means being trustworthy. It includes not plotting harm for your neighbors or neighborhood. It also involves watching out for others without overstepping your boundaries.

As a good neighbor, take some initiative and invite your neighbors over to your home and welcome them with kindness and respect. Be the kind of neighbor you wish you had, and perhaps your neighbors will return the favor. Welcome your neighbors with the love of Jesus and watch the way the Lord can work in your community.

*Lord God, so many times a day You protect me, and I don't even realize it. Thank You! Thank You for the ways You protect and provide. Thank You for the way You flood my mind and my soul with your peace so I can go to bed each night and sleep in peace. Please help me be a safe, trustworthy neighbor to the people who live around me. In Jesus' name I pray, amen.*

## Think It Over

- What are some ways the Lord keeps you safe every day? Thank Him for His protection!
- When you consider the people in your neighborhood, who do you know the best? Who do you trust the most? In an emergency, who would you turn to first?

- How can you be a trustworthy neighbor? What do you need to change? What do you need to continue doing?

## *Put It into Practice*

- Think of one thing you could do to communicate trust to your neighbors. Could it involve getting to know them better? Inviting them over for a get-together? Find a way to establish and deepen your neighborly relationships and begin building trust.

## *Home Work*

Once you make sure you've cleaned all the surfaces in your dining room—or kitchen table or wherever you sit down and eat your meals—it's time to touch up your baseboards and floors. Dust your baseboards, then thoroughly clean your floors, whether you need to mop, sweep, vacuum, or use a carpet cleaner. Also be sure to move the table and chairs to clean up any crumbs that are hiding outside of your line of sight.

# *Helping Others When You Can*

*Do not withhold good from those who deserve it when it's in your power to help them. If you can help your neighbor now, don't say, "Come back tomorrow, and then I'll help you."*

PROVERBS 3:27–28 NLT

How often do people ask you for help? Do you often discover you're helping other people through their challenges more than you focus on your own?

How about your neighbors? How often do they ask you for your help? Do you often find yourself in the middle of another commitment when someone stops by and asks you for help?

Especially when you finally find a teensy bit of free time to tackle your to-do list and someone desperately needs your help, it can be tempting to focus on finishing what you've started. You delay helping others because their issues are so time-consuming. You may reason that as soon as you get your own project finished, you can give your time to someone else.

The Bible invites you to consider a different perspective. Proverbs tells us to act when we're asked—not to delay. Perhaps the author knew how often procrastination turns into inaction.

Woven throughout the Old and New Testament, the greatest commandment is a defining way of life for those who honor and fear the Lord. First and foremost, we're to love the Lord our God with all our hearts, souls, minds, and strength. Secondly, we need to love our neighbors as we love ourselves. You could consider your neighbor to be any person, regardless of where they live. Loving your neighbor could involve loving your family members, your friends, your coworkers, and strangers in the grocery store. But loving your neighbor certainly includes people who live near you.

Who are your actual, physical neighbors? Do you know them by name? Have you tried to get to know them? So often, there are two extremes of neighboring: either getting to know each other very well and frequently being involved in each other's lives, or not knowing each other at all.

What if there could be a happy medium? Think about the possibility of getting to know your neighbors and respecting them, without feeling the need to become best friends forever. Could you get to know them and love them for who they are? Could you show them the love of Jesus by the things you say, the kind things you do, and the way you maintain your property?

Part of loving someone includes helping when you know help is needed. It's taking the time or money or opportunity to reach out and make life easier. As Proverbs 3 advises, it's important to do good by helping people. It's also important to do this right away. Instead of postponing your assistance, help as soon as you can. This sort of thoughtful, loving help involves helping your neighbors when possible. You won't always be able to help, but when you can, do.

By helping your neighbors, especially when they need it the most, you're showing a fantastic and practical way to love well.

*Lord Almighty, You've placed me where I need to be right now. No matter what my home is like, no matter what my neighborhood is like, I'm here for a reason. Please help me be Your representative to my surrounding neighbors. Help me get to know them and be available to help if needed. I want to glorify You with all of my relationships, including those with my neighbors. When I'm tempted to delay helping someone, for whatever reason, please help me make the loving, caring choice. As hard as this seems to ask You, please help me deny my own wishes and be helpful. I want to be more like Jesus. In His name I pray, amen.*

## Think It Over

- How well do you know your actual, physical neighbors? To whom do you need to introduce yourself? When can you make an introduction?
- Have your neighbors ever asked you for help? Have you asked them for help? Do you have an opportunity to help a neighbor right now, or do you need to wait?
- How could you welcome a new neighbor? How could you get to know your current neighbors even better?

## *Put It into Practice*

- You won't be able to help or love your neighbors if you don't know them. Reach out as best as you can and get to know the people who live close to you. Close relationships aren't required but try to know your neighbors by name.

## *Home Work*

Depending on how attentive you are to dusty surfaces, you may be an avid duster, or you may consider dust bunnies to be pets in your home. Take some time to dust surfaces in your dining room, along with any lights, lampshades, or light fixtures in the room. If your dining room has windows, wash them until they shine.

# All Who Come to See

*For two whole years Paul stayed there in his own rented house and welcomed all who came to see him. He proclaimed the kingdom of God and taught about the Lord Jesus Christ—with all boldness and without hindrance!*

Acts 28:30–31

So many factors are part of your willingness or unwillingness to welcome people into your life and your home. Your personality type affects the way you view people in general. Does the thought of spending time with people energize you or deplete your energy? Do you love the thought of talking with a stranger or dread it?

Your basic perception of hospitality also greatly influences your willingness to welcome people. If you've been raised in a home where hospitality is the norm, you're probably quick to invite other people. If you've had bad experiences or simply no hosting experience, inviting and welcoming people into your home may feel scary or even impossible.

Your stage and season of life also contribute to your openness to host others. You might find yourself in a lonely spot in life, and you'd love to have a visitor to keep you company. Or, your days and nights might fly by in a flash, and you have no time to fit anything else into your frantic schedule.

Think through how willing or even excited you are about inviting people into your life and home. What contributes to your willingness? What's affecting your level of excitement?

Sometimes, whether you're willing or not, guests may come to your home. When they do, be prepared to welcome them out of your love for and obedience to Christ. And whenever possible, consider these opportunities for hospitality to be divine appointments. Use them for the glory of God.

One excellent example of this is found in the life of Paul. As a bit of a back story, Paul was arrested in Jerusalem. The ruling power, the Romans, wanted to release him in Jerusalem, but Jews sought his death—so Paul appealed to Caesar and was sent to Rome. When Roman Jews heard about

Paul's arrest in Rome, they were intrigued. So they gathered and brought others with them.

Even when Paul was in chains and under house arrest in Rome, he was allowed to welcome visitors. And welcome visitors he did! All who came to see Paul were welcomed with gospel truth. Not only did he proclaim the kingdom of God but he also boldly taught about the Lord Jesus Christ without hindrance.

Paul was able to explain the truth of the gospel from his own home "from morning till evening" (Acts 28:23). As long as he had an opportunity, he explained the kingdom of God and tried to persuade his visitors about Jesus from the Law of Moses and from the Prophets. For two years, Paul would continue to boldly preach the gospel and about how the Old Testament points to Christ.

The result? Some were convinced about Jesus. Others refused to believe.

Lord willing, you won't be put under house arrest. And most likely, you will not have a huge following of crowds of people. But you can still follow Paul's lead. Welcome all who come to see you, whether the idea of hospitality excites you or not. Dare to proclaim the kingdom of God. Boldly teach about the Lord Jesus Christ.

Like Paul, you can use your home, no matter how modest or extravagant, short-term or long-term, as a place to tell others about Jesus. Let the Word of God resound in your home, whether it's through music you choose to play, your mealtime prayers, or the words you choose to use. May all who come to see you understand more of who Jesus Christ is as they spend time in your presence.

*Lord Jesus, not everyone I know believes that You are the Christ. They haven't accepted You as Savior. I would love for You to use me and my home to point others to You. Please give me boldness to proclaim Your kingdom. Give me words that will clearly explain You to others who need to hear Your truth. I ask all of this in Your holy name, amen.*

## Think It Over

- Do you tend to wait before welcoming others to your home, or are you quick to invite them? Whether you're living somewhere briefly or for a long time, don't overlook your opportunities to show hospitality.
- You may be comfortable in boldly telling others about Christ, just like Paul. Or you might feel more timid. What is your comfort level in sharing your faith with others?
- If you're comfortable proclaiming the kingdom of God, who can you invite to your home next?
- If you're more timid about sharing your faith, what are some ways you could point others to Jesus in the comfort of your home. Could you add something to your surroundings, whether it's artwork or what you display on your refrigerator? Could it be the music you choose to play?

## Put It into Practice

- Think about someone who would be receptive to talking about Jesus. Can you invite this person to your home and have a Christ-centered discussion without hindrance?
- Plan to welcome someone into your home and talk about the truth of the gospel in some way.

## Home Work

Keep preparing your dining area for guests by gathering your table linens. Depending on your personal preference, you may have tablecloths, cloth napkins, place mats, or other table linens around your home. Make sure they're gathered and easy to access when it's time to set the table. If you prefer paper napkins, keep those in a familiar spot, so when guests come over for a meal, you won't have to search your home to find what you need.

# *Welcoming the Marginalized*

Whether it's in your life or in your home, it can seem so easy to welcome people you want to welcome. Jesus taught about this tendency in His Sermon on the Mount: "You have heard that it was said, 'Love your neighbor and hate your enemy.' But I tell you, love your enemies and pray for those who persecute you, that you may be children of your Father in heaven. He causes his sun to rise on the evil and the good, and sends rain on the righteous and the unrighteous. *If you love those who love you, what reward will you get? Are not even the tax collectors doing that? And if you greet only your own people, what are you doing more than others? Do not even pagans do that?*" (Matthew 5:43–47, emphasis mine).

What reward will you get if you welcome only those who welcome you? So many people in this world need the kindness and warmth of your welcome, but you may not even know them. Some of these people can't give you anything in return. Hardships can hit when you least expect them, financially or relationally creating deep wounds. Life can change in a moment, leaving people heartbroken, as widows or orphans.

Life is hard. And when you see that life has become increasingly difficult for someone you know, it's not time to turn away. It's not time to turn your back on the marginalized. Rather, you can provide a listening ear, some understanding, prayers, material help, or a safe haven by opening your life or your home in hospitality. Welcome the marginalized and see how the Lord will use your hospitality to help others.

# Welcoming with Mercy and Compassion

*This is what the LORD Almighty said: "Administer true justice; show mercy and compassion to one another. Do not oppress the widow or the fatherless, the foreigner or the poor. Do not plot evil against each other."*

ZECHARIAH 7:9–10

Do you tend to be a go-getter, always looking for someone to bless or some way to serve? When you hear about a need, do you automatically switch into fix-it mode? Or do you hold back and shelter yourself from opportunities?

Throughout the Bible, the call for those who fear and revere the Lord is consistent: Love the Lord with all your heart, mind, soul, and strength. Love your neighbor too. But loving your neighbor involves more than the people who live nearby, and it involves more than feeling warm fuzzies and compassion. Followers of Christ need to get in the mindset and habit of loving well in word, thought, and action.

The prophet Zechariah shared wise counsel about loving well in word, thought, and action, which encompasses hospitality. If the Lord Almighty wants His followers to administer true justice, we need to submit to His command. If He wants His followers to show mercy and compassion to others, we must obey. If we read God's Word and understand that we shouldn't oppress anyone, whether widows, orphans, foreigners, or the poor, we need to make sure we don't. And if we know that we shouldn't plot evil, we can prevent this by planning good.

One way to show mercy and compassion while caring for widows, orphans, foreigners, and the poor is to befriend them. Get to know people who are different from you. Walk through hard seasons of life with people who are facing heartbreak. Instead of turning away from someone surrounded by difficulty, step into the challenging circumstances with them.

Perhaps one of the easiest ways to do this is to include others who are facing hardship. If you know a woman is grieving the loss of her husband, get involved in her life. Invite her to dinner or go out for coffee together. Ask if you can help her take care of basic tasks around her home. Make sure she knows you're available to help her, if needed, and that you're interested in her well-being. The same is true for those without parents, for people who are alone due to relocation or a big move, or for the needy in your community. And if someone doesn't fit the descriptions in the Bible but you know he or she is struggling with loss or need, choose to be helpful and let your light for Christ shine.

Fortunately, welcoming others isn't restricted to hospitality in your home. It's easily expandable into all of life. You can be welcoming as you ask someone who's alone to sit with you at church. You can make others feel welcome by getting together both within and beyond your home. The invitation and investment in a relationship are the important parts, not your surroundings.

Instead of keeping yourself from those who are hurting or facing life's storms, step into life with them and welcome them into your heart and your home. As you walk through life together, not only will your genuine concern be a blessing to someone in need but you'll also be blessed by conversations and relationships you would miss by insulating yourself within the familiar or comfortable.

As you meet and minister to new people in the name of Jesus, you will receive unimaginable intangible blessings in return, both here on earth and in heaven.

*Lord God, You've placed me at this time in history and in my community for a good reason. Please use me! Show me who needs my care, concern, love, and help the most. I pray I would courageously reach out to the lonely and hurting in my circle of influence. Bring widows and orphans into my life. Show me ways I can welcome foreigners. I want to follow through and welcome! I want to help the needy and poor. And when I get nervous or I hesitate to do it, please change my heart and attitude. Please increase the generosity of my time, resources, and love. Help me love and serve and give without expecting anything in return. In Jesus' name I pray, amen.*

## Think It Over

- Who in your circle of influence is going through a particularly difficult time? How can you step into that world and demonstrate Christ's love?
- How can you show mercy to someone in need? What are some practical ways you could be more compassionate to someone?
- How could you bless the life of a widow? How could you bless an orphan? Once you think of what you'd like to do, when will you reach out and act?
- How can you welcome foreigners in your community?
- What are you doing right now to help the poor in your area? How can you increase your help?

## Put It into Practice

- Reflect on everything you've just considered; when will you put all of your helpful ideas into action? How and when can you get started?
- Who is the first person you'll reach out to help? Make the call. Send the text or email. Start making connections now.

## Home Work

If you can spend time cleaning only two rooms before company comes, focus your work on your kitchen and bathroom. For now, clean off and wipe down your bathroom countertops. If you have multiple bathrooms, try to clean all of them. While you're cleaning your countertops, wipe down your bathroom sinks and clean all faucets.

# Settled in a Home

*Father of the fatherless and protector of widows is God in his holy habitation. God settles the solitary in a home; he leads out the prisoners to prosperity, but the rebellious dwell in a parched land.*

Psalm 68:5–6 ESV

The Lord is amazing. He is completely righteous and holy, all-knowing and all-powerful. He could do absolutely anything He fancies, yet out of His faithful and constant love, He chooses to care for His children who can't care for themselves. He watches over and nurtures the orphan. He provides for and protects the widow. He prospers the prisoner. And He settles the solitary in a home.

The Lord looks past outward appearances to see each person's heart; He knows everyone's deepest needs. And He faithfully meets the needs of His own. He knows orphans need a father, so He steps into their lives to lovingly protect them in ways they may or may not see. He knows widows lack the protection of a husband, so He steps in to provide. He knows the longing in the heart of the solitary, and He establishes what they most need: a home. And He gives prisoners prosperity in unexpected ways.

Because God is the giver of all good gifts—every good and perfect gift comes from Him (James 1:17)—we can try to follow His example.

When He brings an orphan into our lives, we can look for ways to help in a parental sense. Ask thoughtful, caring questions. Begin a mentoring relationship, whether formal or informal. Look for opportunities to invite the orphan into your home, whether for a simple meal or a holiday gathering.

As you get to know widows and widowers, find opportunities to include and help them. Do they need a little extra help around their houses? Could you accompany them to a doctor's appointment or to the store? Are they celebrating the holidays with anyone, or will they be home alone?

Think about those who are lonely—the solitary souls in your life. Who are they? How well do you know them? How can you reach out to them? They may or may not be established in their own homes, but everyone's life is better with more friendly influences. How could you get to know them better?

Finally, think about prisoners. This may mean people who are actually incarcerated, or you could widen your scope to consider people who are imprisoned in some sort of addiction, illness, or abusive situation. How can you reach out in the love of Christ and help? Compassion and counseling may be natural strengths of yours, and you can use these gifts to help others in need. However, if you're not comfortable with counseling, what kind of organizations could use your assistance, whether it's your time, other talents, or treasure?

As you begin to include the marginalized in your life, sometimes it may involve your home. Opening your home to loved ones you know are going through difficult times can be a practical way to bring comfort. Surroundings that are familiar to you might provide a powerful solace to those who truly feel alone.

If you find yourself in a lonely, or solitary, season of life, you can use the home the Lord has given you for His glory. Use your time and resources to reach out to others. As you welcome them into your life and home, you'll glorify the Lord and also enrich your own life and the lives of the people you welcome.

*Lord God, You are so good. The way You care for people is so loving and kind. The way You meet the needs of Your children is so generous. Thank You! It's such a relief to know that no matter what situation I find myself in, You will sustain me. You will comfort me and provide. As long as I'm able, please use me to bless others. I want to be used by You to step in and help those who are all alone. Please show me opportunities and give me boldness to care and love others well. In Jesus' name I pray, amen.*

## Think It Over

- What solitary men, women, and children do you know? How can you begin to reach out to them in kindness?
- If you already have a close relationship with a widow, orphan, or prisoner, what blessings have you experienced? How about challenges? What

blessings and challenges have they experienced since you've been part of their lives?

- Look at your calendar and see when you could spend time with those who could use your company. What could you do to bless them?

## *Put It into Practice*

- Often, it's easier to think of people who are alone than to actually reach out to help them. Instead of merely talking about helping, it's time to do something. Who will you reach out to this week? How will you reach out?

## *Home Work*

Where do you keep your medicine and toiletries? It's time to clean this area! Get rid of expired or almost empty containers, then organize the rest. Aside from perishable products you use (or haven't used), clean any accessories you use to care for yourself, like toothbrushes and dental floss, or tools like thermometers and heating pads. Next time you need them, either for yourself or a guest, you'll know where everything is!

# Welcoming the Weary in Jesus' Name

*Paul and Barnabas disagreed with them, arguing vehemently. Finally, the church decided to send Paul and Barnabas to Jerusalem, accompanied by some local believers, to talk to the apostles and elders about this question. The church sent the delegates to Jerusalem, and they stopped along the way in Phoenicia and Samaria to visit the believers. They told them—much to everyone's joy—that the Gentiles, too, were being converted. When they arrived in Jerusalem, Barnabas and Paul were welcomed by the whole church, including the apostles and elders. They reported everything God had done through them.*

Acts 15:2–4 NLT

Facing conflict with other people can be a very draining, painful challenge. It's especially discouraging when you have no idea when or how the conflict might be resolved. Whether you disagree with someone you know very well or someone you barely know, trying to work through differences can be difficult. Not only does conflict leave you feeling down but it also can deplete you of energy and encouragement.

Paul and Barnabas were doing the Lord's work, but not everything was smooth sailing for them. They battled opposition from Jews and Gentiles, but members of the early church also disagreed with them. Words hurt and disagreements stung, even for these giants of the faith. While they trusted the Lord to guide their words and attitudes, the conflict must have been draining.

After the church couldn't come to an agreement with Paul and Barnabas, they sent the men away to talk about matters with the apostles and elders. The two men didn't make a beeline to Jerusalem in silence and seclusion, though. On their journey to Jerusalem, Paul and Barnabas stopped along the way to visit believers. Even in the middle of conflict, they appreciated the welcoming hospitality of believers in Phoenicia and Samaria.

Once they made it to their destination in Jerusalem, they enjoyed more hospitality. Even though they were weary from their long journey and worn out by disagreeing with their brothers and sisters in Christ, the entire church in Jerusalem welcomed them.

Welcome was what these two servant leaders needed. And their arrival brought great joy as believers all along the way, from Phoenicia to Samaria to Jerusalem, were happy to hear the news from Paul and Barnabas that Gentiles were coming to know the Lord.

Just as Paul and Barnabas might have been worn out by life—whether it was their constant, consistent ministry or disagreeing with church members or making a long journey—there's no doubt they would've found encouragement, refreshment, and joy through everyone's warm welcomes.

In a similar way, you may not know of the people in your life who currently face draining challenges. They may need the warmth of your welcome and the refreshment of your hospitality. The wonderful news is that you have the resources to make a difference in someone's difficult journey. Through your kindness and gentleness, you can foster healing and rest. Through the comfort of your home, you can offer peace and restoration. And through your conversations and caring questions, you can encourage purpose and help others process difficult thoughts and feelings.

Whether you realize it or not, your intentional hospitality can transform your home into a type of holy hospital, where those who are battered and broken by this world come for a visit and leave feeling rested and restored. The key is to prayerfully invite guests to your home and minister to them in a way that acts as a balm to their souls. That's truly a fantastic way to use your home and your ability to welcome.

*Lord God, thank You for creating hospitality and welcomes. Thank You for the power that a welcome has to change and refresh the weariest of souls. Thank You for welcoming me into Your family through Jesus. I want to spread His love to others around me—especially people who are facing difficult times. Please reveal to me who I need to reach out to in Christian compassion. Please give me time and energy and courage to invite others into my home so that I may love them well. In Jesus' name I pray, amen.*

## Think It Over

- Who in your life needs refreshing? Who is going through a particularly difficult time? You don't necessarily need to host overnight guests—making a difference could be as easy as inviting people over for coffee and a conversation.
- In what ways have people blessed you in the past with their welcome when you needed it the most?
- What are some of your favorite ways to dote on visitors to your home? How are you known for showing your kindness?

## Put It into Practice

- When the Lord brings someone to mind, reach out to that person. Be willing to ask the tough questions to see how life is going. And when you feel the tug to open your home, don't delay. Make the invitation. Make a difference for someone who needs your kindness.

## Home Work

Now that you've cleaned your medicine cabinet in your bathroom (or elsewhere), it's time to tackle your vanity, including all of your personal care products. Whether you store your personal care products in a cabinet, drawer, shelf, or somewhere else, sort your stash. Toss the expired products, along with items you know you won't use again. Organize all of your hair care, makeup, or any other tools you might use. This chore is much less about making spaces presentable for your guests, and much more about cleaning up every aspect of specific rooms.

# *What Are You Waiting For?*

*Jesus went on to say, "To what, then, can I compare the people of this generation? What are they like? They are like children sitting in the marketplace and calling out to each other:*

*'We played the pipe for you,*
*and you did not dance;*
*we sang a dirge,*
*and you did not cry.'*

*For John the Baptist came neither eating bread nor drinking wine, and you say, 'He has a demon.' The Son of Man came eating and drinking, and you say, 'Here is a glutton and a drunkard, a friend of tax collectors and sinners.'"*

Luke 7:31–34

This might seem obvious, but your guests may be very different from what you expect or imagine them to be like.

While it's evident that every person has free will, a unique personality, and the responsibility for his or her choices, sometimes you might fall into a trap of thinking you are the one who knows what's best. Perhaps you think you know how a guest will respond. Maybe you've thought of what another person *should* say. Or you think you know a person so well that you have imagined exactly what she will do.

Be careful with your expectations and preconceived ideas, because you might be very surprised by what actually happens.

This definitely was the case during Jesus' life on earth. It might have seemed like the religious elite would have gladly welcomed the Son of God into their synagogues and communities. Here was the long-awaited Messiah who clearly fulfilled prophecy after prophecy. Yet Jewish leaders didn't believe Him. They didn't recognize Him. And they didn't welcome Him.

Part of the reason was that Jesus wasn't exactly what they expected. As

Jesus pointed out, the religious leaders of His day turned away John the Baptist, thinking the prophet was demon-possessed. And they judged Jesus because He ate, drank, and spent time with sinners and outcasts.

Stuck in their own presuppositions and preconceived ideas, the religious leaders of Jesus' day missed out on welcoming the Savior of the world.

May we not repeat their mistakes. When given the opportunity to welcome others into our churches or our homes, may we do so with open hearts and open minds. May we not be so quick to judge, but rather look for glimpses of truth and listen to the heart of what's being said.

We may not be able to physically welcome the Son of God, but think about what Jesus taught in Matthew 25:34–40 (ESV):

> Then the King will say to those on his right, "Come, you who are blessed by my Father, inherit the kingdom prepared for you from the foundation of the world. For I was hungry and you gave me food, I was thirsty and you gave me drink, I was a stranger and you welcomed me, I was naked and you clothed me, I was sick and you visited me, I was in prison and you came to me." Then the righteous will answer Him, saying, "Lord, when did we see you hungry and feed you, or thirsty and give you drink? And when did we see you a stranger and welcome you, or naked and clothe you? And when did we see you sick or in prison and visit you?" And the King will answer them, "Truly, I say to you, as you did it to one of the least of these my brothers, you did it to me."

Learning from Christ, when you discern that someone is a fellow believer, welcome your brother or sister in Christ!

If your guest communicates that she is an unbeliever, look for opportunities to gently and respectfully give a reason for your hope (1 Pet. 3:15).

And if you're unsure where your guest stands or what she believes, pray for discernment. Be wise as serpents yet innocent as doves (Matt. 10:16).

Apart from your expectations of other people, be cautious about creating your own expectations for Jesus. Do you think the Lord should work in a particular way? Are you disappointed or frustrated when He doesn't do what you think He should? Guard against those attitudes. Prepare yourself to welcome Jesus, who brings surprises into your everyday life.

*Father, please forgive me for holding unrealistic expectations of others. Please help me show grace to others. I want to be welcoming in how I act and talk so that others don't feel turned away by me. I want to live a righteous life in Your eyes without expecting everyone around me to be righteous. Please help me to gently, kindly, and effectively point others to Jesus. Let Jesus be the one to change a person's heart and mind, not me. He is the only one to bring complete transformation. It's in His name I pray, amen.*

## Think It Over

- How often do you find other people either fall short of your expectations or exceed them? What does this reveal about your expectations?
- How often do you find yourself surprising other people? Are you ever surprised by the expectations other people have for you?
- What kind of expectations do you have for Jesus? How have you noticed that He is different from what you expect?
- How might your hospitality and hosting practices change if you extend grace to your guests and give them the freedom to be themselves?

## Put It into Practice

- Welcome others into your home without any expectations. Instead of falling into the trap of having people never measure up to what you expect, let them surprise you.

## Home Work

It can be amazing to see how much dust gathers in a bathroom! Take time to dust everything, from the toilet paper holder to the bathroom lights and shower head. After you've dusted everything, wash your bathroom windows and mirrors. This could be a great time to clean any window coverings or shower curtains as well.

# *Welcomed in Sickness and in Health*

*As you know, it was because of an illness that I first preached the gospel to you, and even though my illness was a trial to you, you did not treat me with contempt or scorn. Instead, you welcomed me as if I were an angel of God, as if I were Christ Jesus himself.*

Galatians 4:13–14

Fair-weather fans exist in sports—and in everyday life. You know the kind of friends who are happiest and most involved in your life when everything's going well. But when sickness or any sort of crisis pops up, where do your fair-weather friends go? You may never hear from them again. It's a real-life portrayal of Proverbs 19:4: "Wealth makes many 'friends'; poverty drives them all away" (NLT).

Life is challenging, and every relationship is filled with highs and lows, closeness and distance. However, you can thank the Lord for the women and men in your life who refuse to disappear when times get tough. It's a gift when you're able to lean on reliable friends and family members who are there for you no matter what. Receiving encouragement and support when you need it most is priceless.

When you find your people—the ones who stick with you during good and bad times—be sure to tell them how much you appreciate them. In whatever way works best for you and them, communicate your love and respect.

Paul found his group of support in the church of Galatia. While he spent time with his brothers and sisters in Christ, he had gotten sick. Instead of being upset about the inconvenience and trouble Paul's sickness caused, the Galatians welcomed him. In sickness and in health they honored Paul just like they would have honored Christ.

No doubt, the Galatian welcome struck a deep chord with Paul, because he remembered his sickness and their gracious and caring welcome. While the Galatian church ministered to his sick body, they ended up ministering to his soul as well.

People will enter and exit your life. If you wait long enough, your dear friends and family members will get sick and go through unthinkable trials. While it will hurt to see them suffer and endure, you have a unique opportunity to be a shining light, sweet encouragement, and a comforting help.

Like the Galatian church, make sure your sick loved ones feel loved and not slighted. Treat your loved ones just as you would treat Jesus if He were right here with you. Remember that whatever you do for others, as humble or as helpless as they may be, you're doing it for Christ.

What you do and how you treat others truly matters, even and especially when no one else is watching. Instead of being a fair-weather friend, make sure to welcome your sick loved ones just as you would welcome Jesus.

*Father, I want to mirror Christ in my sacrificial love for others. I want to be known as someone who follows through and lives out what I believe. I don't want to be a big talker, and I don't want to be a fair-weather friend. Please show me how I can help my friends and family members who are facing difficult challenges. Please help me to welcome and love with action and deeds just as You would. In Jesus' name I pray, amen.*

## Think It Over

- When have you been hurt by a fair-weather friend? When have you been blessed by the dedication and love of a true friend?
- What is one of the most sacrificial or kind ways you've helped a friend or family member in need?
- How could you love someone well? Brainstorm ways to show compassion and care for others who are dealing with life's challenges.
- What can you do now to help a family member or friend who is in the greatest need?

## Put It into Practice

- All of the good intentions in the world don't mean a thing if they never turn into action. It's time to turn your good ideas into good deeds. This week, take time to bless someone in need!

## *Home Work*

Once the hidden areas of your bathroom are cleaned, it's time to work on the more noticeable spots. Take time to deep clean your toilet. Scrub the bowl, the rim, the seat, the tank, and the base. Spray with a cleaner, scrub if needed, and then wipe everything down. Just about everyone will appreciate a clean toilet!

# *Welcoming in Surprise*

Surprise! Has anyone thrown you a surprise party? How did you feel as the guest of honor? Here's another question: Have you ever welcomed someone into your home when you least expected it? Maybe people just dropped by for a visit, or maybe they gave you a couple hours' notice before coming over. How did you feel when you became a surprise host?

When it comes to hospitality, sometimes you get the opportunity to plan what you would like to host and invite guests of your choosing. Other times, people invite themselves to your home or completely surprise you with a visit.

While it might seem easier to welcome guests you invited or intended to host, the real test of your friendliness and welcome comes when you're thrown into hospitality at a moment's notice. What do you do when your hospitality comes as a surprise?

Granted, sometimes your surprise guests could have let you know in advance. But other times, if your guests happen to unexpectedly pass through your neighborhood and their schedules free up, you might get a visit. Either way, your true heart for hospitality gets thrown on display.

The Bible is filled with stories of unsuspecting hosts and how these men and women welcomed their visitors with attitudes and actions that glorified God. May we learn from their examples and also find ways to honor the Lord with our welcoming homes and welcoming attitudes, even when the opportunities come as complete surprises.

# How Unexpected Visitors Can Change Your Life

*Now a priest of Midian had seven daughters, and they came to draw water and fill the troughs to water their father's flock. Some shepherds came along and drove them away, but Moses got up and came to their rescue and watered their flock. When the girls returned to Reuel their father, he asked them, "Why have you returned so early today?" They answered, "An Egyptian rescued us from the shepherds. He even drew water for us and watered the flock." "And where is he?" Reuel asked his daughters. "Why did you leave him? Invite him to have something to eat." Moses agreed to stay with the man, who gave his daughter Zipporah to Moses in marriage.*

Exodus 2:16–21

Think about your favorite people in your life. You met every single one of them at some point. At one moment you didn't know each other. Then you met and your lives were never the same. Considering this perspective, it can and should be exciting to meet new people, because you're never sure exactly how long they'll be a part of your life. Some people come and go quickly, but others? They might stay in your life much longer than you'd ever imagine.

This was the case with Reuel and his daughter Zipporah. After a normal day of household chores, Zipporah and her sisters met a kind stranger who rescued them from some surly shepherds. Even after this stranger saved the day, Zipporah and her sisters headed home—but when they told their dad what had happened, the family returned to invite the kind man for dinner.

Little did the stranger, Moses, know that Zipporah would end up as his wife and the mother of his children.

Moses' life had been anything but boring. From his parents' choice to disobey Pharaoh and keep him, their son, alive to his adoption by Pharaoh's daughter, his childhood was extraordinary. Even after spending his childhood growing up in Pharaoh's household, Moses knew he was a Hebrew.

And when he watched an Egyptian beat a fellow Hebrew, Moses retaliated in murder.

The crime he thought he had committed in secret became known. And when the Hebrews found out he killed an Egyptian, Moses fled from Egypt to Midian. While there, he happened upon the daughters of Reuel, the Midianite priest, and defended them.

Not only did Reuel repay Moses with a grateful invitation and a meal but he ended up asking Moses to stay and marry his daughter Zipporah. What a welcome!

Life has a funny way of twisting and turning unexpectedly. Imagine the surprise of Moses, Reuel, and Zipporah. Moses fled Egypt for his life and the sake of his reputation. Surely his spirits would have been low, as he was on the run. But when he chose to do what was right and defend Reuel's daughters from the shepherds, he won the welcome and favor of Reuel. In the end, he gained a wife as a result of his good deed.

Truly, you never know what your spur-of-the-moment choices may lead to. And you never know what might happen as a result of welcoming people into your home. But instead of trying to figure out every possible outcome, simply trust the Lord and offer your hospitality. Perhaps your invitation may end with one well-intentioned and well-received meal. Or perhaps your welcome will affect generations to come. The only way you'll find out is by extending an invitation.

*Father, thank You for the creative ways You bring people into my life. I never know who You might bring my way and how my life will be changed. May I remember that everyone in my life was new to me at some point. Please use that to inspire and encourage me to meet others. Being friendly and welcoming to others glorifies You. No matter what my personality may prefer, please help me to be loving and kind as a way to demonstrate my faith and devotion to You. In Jesus' name I pray, amen.*

## Think It Over

- You never know where a chance meeting will lead. Think about one person in your life today whom you met in an exceptionally unique way. What was your encounter like? What ended up happening as a result?
- How important do you think first impressions are? Who left a good first impression on you? Who left a bad first impression?
- When did you know that you needed to invite someone to your home to say thank you? How did you extend that invitation? What happened as a result of your hospitality?
- Zipporah and her sisters left Moses at the well. It wasn't until their father insisted on hosting Moses that they extended an invitation. Are you quick to realize opportunities to offer hospitality, like Reuel? Or do you need prompting, like Zipporah?

## Put It into Practice

- You've met every single person in your life at some point, and you never know who may remain in your life for years to come. Consider these truths as you meet new people. As you introduce yourself to others, treat them genuinely and with kindness.

## Home Work

To prepare your home for company, spend time scrubbing out your bathroom sink. Make sure it's all clean. You've already focused on cleaning any countertops in your bathroom; now's your time to deep clean your actual sink! Depending on how messy or neatly people in your home wash their hands or brush their teeth, you may also need to wipe down nearby walls to clean up any splatter messes.

# Spur-of-the-Moment Hospitality

*Abigail acted quickly. She took two hundred loaves of bread, two skins of wine, five dressed sheep, five seahs of roasted grain, a hundred cakes of raisins and two hundred cakes of pressed figs, and loaded them on donkeys. Then she told her servants, "Go on ahead; I'll follow you." But she did not tell her husband Nabal. When Abigail saw David, she quickly got off her donkey and bowed down before David with her face to the ground. "And let this gift, which your servant has brought to my lord, be given to the men who follow you."*

1 Samuel 25:18–19, 23, 27

Have you ever needed to prepare a meal or your home for an important guest at the last minute? Do you remember how much you searched your cupboards to throw together a meal that was just right? Did you rush around making sure your home was presentable? Do you remember the surge of adrenaline as you rushed to prepare?

In the Old Testament, Abigail knew the manic rush. But it all could have been avoided. If you've ever read about Abigail and her less-than-desirable husband, Nabal, you know that Abigail's life was filled with challenges. As 1 Samuel 25:3 describes, "She was an intelligent and beautiful woman, but her husband was surly and mean in his dealings."

Because Abigail's bad-tempered husband put her in unfavorable situations, she had to right Nabal's wrongs to protect herself and her household. When one of her servants reported how poorly Nabal had treated David and his men, the servant sought out Abigail's help, saying: "Now think it over and see what you can do, because disaster is hanging over our master and his whole household. He is such a wicked man that no one can talk to him" (1 Sam. 25:17).

Abigail jumped into problem-solving mode and tried to smooth things over with a huge dose of quick thinking and generous hospitality. Right away, she decided that choice food and a warm welcome might be enough to change David's mind. Together with her servants, Abigail attempted to avert the impending disaster with much bread and wine, figs and raisins, sheep and roasted grain.

Delivering this feast to David and his men, Abigail showed respect and reverence to David without her husband's knowledge. She wisely chose to attempt to right her husband's wrongs. The result? David spared Nabal's household. (As 1 Samuel 25:38 recounts, ten days later the Lord struck Nabal and he died, and David took Abigail as his wife.)

Hopefully, you don't have to deal with someone like Nabal in your life. But there are times when, like Abigail, you need to think fast, make quick decisions, and jump into action. If you need to smooth over rocky situations, consider offering some hospitality. How can you use your warm welcome to mend relationships? How can delicious food and drink soften hearts and soothe hurts?

Spur-of-the-moment hospitality may not be easy. It might add a lot more stress to your life as you consider quick, resourceful choices. But it can make a huge difference and act as a healing balm to fractured relationships and less-than-ideal situations.

*Lord, You know the way food ministers to a person. You created people this way! And You created the gift of taste and delicious food. I pray I will never be put in a situation like Abigail's, where I need to think quickly to save my household. But I ask that when I need to make speedy decisions that You would give me wisdom and discernment. Please help me be resourceful and generous with all that You've given me. It's a relief to know I can trust you in sticky situations. Please help me be willing to welcome others even if it seems to happen when I least expect it. In Jesus' name I pray, amen.*

## Think It Over

- What is one way you could use your hospitality to mend difficult relationships in your life?
- Why do you think food has a way of ministering to people and smoothing over rough patches? How have you watched this happen in your own life?
- Do you currently have any strained relationships that could benefit from your taking a step toward reconciliation?

- Abigail's picnic feast for David and his men would have come at a great cost. Yet she was resourceful, a quick thinker, and knew how to make it happen. Think through a go-to menu for a company-ready meal. What can you serve others if you ever need some last-minute hospitality?

## *Put It Into Practice*

- Once you consider what to serve your guests, it's time to prepare by doing a little shopping. The next time you're at the grocery store, pick up some ingredients so you're prepared just in case you need to create a spur-of-the-moment meal. You can store the ingredients in a special spot in your kitchen. If no guests show up as the expiration dates approach, enjoy the meal on your own!

## *Home Work*

Your bathroom is almost all clean! Now's the time to focus on cleaning your bathtub or shower. Or both. Take time to really scrub what needs scrubbing. Work on all the soap scum, and don't forget to clean your shower head and faucet. Even if your company isn't spending the night or using your bathtub or shower, spending time on this chore gives you the gift of a clean bathroom. Instead of focusing on cleaning rooms only for other people, enjoy taking time to deep clean your home so that you can enjoy an attractive and clean living space.

Devotion 34

# *Hosting Long-Term Visitors*

*One more thing—please prepare a guest room for me, for I am hoping that God will answer your prayers and let me return to you soon.*

PHILEMON 22 NLT

Have you ever invited yourself to someone else's home? Or has anyone surprised you by inviting themselves over to your home? Was the invitation something you had hoped for and gladly welcomed, or did it make you feel a little uncomfortable? For you, did you notice a difference in your level of excitement or anticipation if you had a close relationship either with your host or your guest?

Depending on the familiarity of your relationship, people may mention in passing that you should visit sometime. Or, if you live out of town, they may tell you that you're always welcome to stay with them. These offers may be completely sincere. And depending on your potential host, your visit may be completely anticipated. Both you and your host might count down the days until you can see each other again.

But other times, invitations may be made out of politeness only. Frankly, an offer to host might even include a subconscious hope that there will never be a follow-through. When a guest does take you up on your offer, the surprise and preparation can add stress.

Because of his close walk with the Holy Spirit, Paul didn't shy away from saying or doing what the Lord prompted him to do—especially in his letters. So when Paul wrote to Philemon about forgiving and welcoming back Philemon's former slave Onesimus, he didn't end his letter with the plea for reconciliation and restoration. Paul requested that Philemon would host him when he finally came to visit. Unfortunately, we have no way of knowing if Philemon welcomed Paul to stay.

People may be kind and offer to host you for an overnight or extended visit. You may be kind and offer to host others. While invitations may never work out, sometimes guests do show up. You may accept an offer for a place to stay. Houseguests may visit you for a night, or longer. Some guests become residents of your home if they stay for months (or years) at a time.

While some of your opportunities to host overnight guests may be true blessings, both for you and your guests, extended stays can bring challenges. As Benjamin Franklin knew, visitors, like fish, stink after three days. Sharing your personal space can make you feel good at first, but after a while all the togetherness gets to be a bit much for everyone.

We have no idea how long Paul typically stayed with his hosts as he traveled. We have no idea what customs were used for travel or hospitality during the first century. Today, however, short visits seem preferable. Avoiding overstaying one's welcome is a polite rule of thumb. Some guests truly need a place to stay, though, and end up visiting for a while. As long as it's mutually beneficial or enjoyable for both the host and the guest, the stay can be a great opportunity.

Biblically speaking, believers are called to fulfill the law of Christ by bearing each other's burdens (Gal. 6:2). What might that look like in a hosting scenario? It could mean facing the uncomfortable reality of boarding long-term guests.

You may never be asked to share your home for an extended period of time—or you may. If you do, one way to navigate emotions and moods is to look at it as a God-given opportunity to make memories and learn lessons while you generously show the love of Christ and act as His ambassador by offering hospitality to someone in need.

*Father God, You have a way of using all kinds of situations and people to teach me lessons and shape me to become more and more like Your Son. If You're preparing me to welcome a long-term guest, please help me learn from You. And if I'll unknowingly become a long-term guest, I pray You will help me be a blessing to my hosts. In any kind of extended-stay scenario, I pray for strength, endurance, kindness, and love for all who are involved. In Jesus' name I pray, amen.*

## Think It Over

- Have you ever been a long-term guest in someone's home? How long did you stay? What do you remember about your experience?
- Have you ever hosted a long-term guest in your home? How long did your visitor stay? What do you remember about your experience?
- What are some challenges that come with extended stays?
- When it comes to extended stays, what have been some blessings you've witnessed?
- Is your home ready for a potential long-term visitor? Is your heart ready?

## Put It into Practice

- Depending on your current season of life and your current living situation, you may or may not be well-suited to host a long-term guest. If you are, start preparing now just in case the Lord brings someone your way.

## Home Work

Your bathroom should look and feel really clean by now. The only major task that's left is cleaning your floor. Start by wiping down your baseboards, then scrub the floor. Most likely you'll need to mop it to truly clean it, but depending on your floor covering, you may need to stick to sweeping, or even vacuuming. However you need to clean your bathroom floor, take time to do it!

# Vouching for a Visitor

*It seems you lost Onesimus for a little while so that you could have him back forever. He is no longer like a slave to you. He is more than a slave, for he is a beloved brother, especially to me. Now he will mean much more to you, both as a man and as a brother in the Lord. So if you consider me your partner, welcome him as you would welcome me. If he has wronged you in any way or owes you anything, charge it to me.*

PHILEMON 15–18 NLT

How many times have you underestimated a person or discovered that you had a completely wrong perception about someone?

Thinking you've figured someone out only to be completely wrong can be pretty surprising. It's nothing new in relationships though. Speaking of misunderstandings and wrong perceptions, Paul's brief letter to Philemon centers on one subject: changing a wrong impression. You see, Paul asked his friend Philemon to accept his friend Onesimus.

While in prison, Paul got to know Onesimus, who had been Philemon's slave. Paul ended up introducing Onesimus to Christ. As a new believer, Onesimus became Paul's son in the faith.

Whatever happened between Philemon and Onesimus in the past, Paul asked for it to be forgiven and forgotten. Vouching for the transformed character of Onesimus, Paul praised the new believer's usefulness and help. Paul even asked Philemon to not think of Onesimus as a servant or slave, but as a brother in the Lord.

Considering the time in history when Paul made this request, most likely it was revolutionary to consider a slave a free man and an equal. Judging from Paul's choice of words, Onesimus lost Philemon's favor or trust in some way in the past: "It seems you lost Onesimus for a little while so that you could have him back forever," (v. 15) and "If he has wronged you in any way or owes you anything, charge it to me" (v. 18). He asked Philemon for a favor and waited for Philemon's response.

We never get to find out if Philemon welcomed Onesimus back. But we do know that we may be put in a similar situation. If you've been wronged, chances are you may need to grant forgiveness and seek reconciliation. An unbiased third party might step in to help your situation, as Paul did.

You may find yourself needing to welcome someone back into your life or your home, as Philemon perhaps welcomed Onesimus or like the father welcomed the prodigal son in Jesus' parable, found in Luke 15. If so, you may feel overjoyed to welcome a loved one back. Or the situation might feel tense and awkward.

On the other hand, you might need to be restored to someone. You may be alienated and need to wait to be welcomed back. If you've wronged someone, you may need to humbly apologize and mend your relationship.

In either situation, whether you need to do the welcoming or you need to be welcomed, pray. Pray for the Lord to restore the situation. Pray for awkwardness to disappear. Pray for complete and total reconciliation.

And if the day comes when you can be reunited and your relationship is restored, know that asking for or granting forgiveness may be necessary and good. Continue to cover the entire situation with prayer as a way to navigate all the intense feelings.

A welcome can be a very good thing, especially when reconciliation is involved. Look at the bright side and pray for the Lord's good favor.

*Father, conflict is so frustrating. Yet it's a normal part of everyday life. Please humble my heart. Remind me that through Christ I've been forgiven for so much. Please help me forgive others like I've been forgiven. And if I've wronged someone, please open my eyes so I can see and ask for forgiveness. I want to restore my broken relationships, Lord. I want to seek reconciliation. Please help me! In Jesus' name I pray, amen.*

## Think It Over

- Do you need someone to welcome you back? Who is it? Is there anything you can do to encourage the process?
- Do you need to welcome someone back? Who is it? What is standing in your way?
- Often, when there's a strained relationship, reconciliation can feel out of

place and uncomfortable. Both parties need humility to help smooth the situation over. Begin praying now for humbled hearts that come to an agreement.

## *Put It into Practice*

- If you're at odds with anyone, it's time to attempt to restore the relationship. Do you need to seek someone out? Is an apology needed? Take the time now to attempt to make things right.

## *Home Work*

If overnight guests come frequently, you'll want to gather some bathroom essentials to make them feel right at home. Think about what guest towels your company can use, as well as if you'd like to offer a fluffy robe or slippers. While that's not at all necessary, if you have the extra storage space in your home, it could be a very welcome touch. As you're making plans and preparations for your overnight guests, find some soap, shampoo, toothpaste, and toothbrushes to offer just in case they forget a necessity while packing.

## Section Nine

# *Moving Past Hospitality Hang-Ups*

You may know that you should be welcoming to others. You may feel compelled to become more hospitable and invite more people to your home. But actually doing it? Well, that's a different story.

There's a huge difference between planning a gathering and actually following through with it, turning your big ideas into an actual welcome. Plenty of obstacles may stand in your way.

You may want to welcome people into your home, but if you struggle with people-pleasing tendencies, it's almost like you get stage fright before you make any invitation.

If you're more concerned about what your home looks like or what to serve or what your guests think of you, there's a chance you can get frozen with fear of disappointing others. Instead of working past it, you may want to wait until everything seems perfect. (Spoiler alert: Because of reality, you will never have a perfect time, the perfect place, or a perfect opportunity.)

Hospitality might seem like a great sacrifice for you—one that you're not willing to make. Opening your home to others might seem like too much, whether it's because of your current season of life or your personality.

Speaking of your personality, if you're prone to worrying, your concerns about all of the hospitality what-ifs may stall your efforts. You can experience freedom, though, and provide a warm welcome when you choose to put your concerns aside and work through your worries.

Finally, dwelling on your hospitality weaknesses is a surefire way to experience less-than-ideal hospitality. Why? You'll get so wrapped up in what you think *could* go wrong that you miss out on what is actually going well.

Turn your weaknesses over to the Lord. Pray and ask Him for help. As you focus on His strength, He'll transform the way you welcome others.

# *Dealing with Weaknesses in Hosting*

*Each time he said, "My grace is all you need. My power works best in weakness." So now I am glad to boast about my weaknesses, so that the power of Christ can work through me.*

2 Corinthians 12:9 NLT

Every person has strengths and weaknesses. It can feel really comfortable to focus on your strengths; it also can be beneficial to get stronger in your natural giftings.

However, there's a lot to be said for working through your weaknesses, no matter how uncomfortable it might feel. This is especially true when your weak areas are aspects of the Christian life. Just because you don't feel like you're gifted to do a particular thing, it doesn't mean you're excused from a specific task.

For example, you may not feel like you have the spiritual gift of evangelism, yet all believers should prioritize the Great Commission to make disciples, baptize, and teach others to observe all Christ commanded. You may not feel like encouragement and giving are your strengths, but you still need to encourage others. You still need to give.

Paul was all too familiar with working through his weaknesses. While he had plenty of strengths, he was also human. He had weaknesses. Instead of feeling constrained by his weaknesses or using them as an excuse, he knew that when the Lord gave him opportunities, he could confidently take anything on, whether he was working out of his personal strengths or weaknesses.

Time and time again, the Lord showed Paul that He was the one who would provide the strength. Not Paul. All Paul needed was to be willing and obedient. The Lord would handle the rest.

Interestingly, the Lord's power works best in weakness—not in someone's strength. While it seems counterintuitive to consider yourself strongest when you feel like you're at your weakest, this is the fascinating reality of a life lived in Christ.

When you feel like you have absolutely nothing to offer, that's the time you can trust in the Lord's power and strength. You don't have to figure out a way to do something on your own. You can still glorify Him. Trust Him to strengthen you, then follow through in obedience. He'll give you strength.

When it comes to trusting in the Lord to provide strength and ability to do the unimaginable, consider how this could affect your hospitality.

If you feel like you're less than excited to invite or host someone, trust the Lord to give you love and kindness in welcoming your guest.

Feeling completely unmotivated, uncomfortable, or unwilling to host company? Tell the Lord through prayer. Confess all your hesitancy and ask Him to work through your issues and attitudes.

When you feel less than confident about your cooking ability or the size or condition of your home, confess your doubts and fears to the Lord. Ask Him to work and watch the way He multiplies your space, your resources, and even your creativity.

If, in the middle of preparations for company, you feel completely swamped and you don't have any idea how you'll get everything done in time, pray as you work. Release the situation to your heavenly Father. Ask for His help.

As Jesus promised, His grace is sufficient for you. It's all you need. His power will be perfected in your weakness. You may be surprised at the exact ways He works, but trust Him. Pray. Tell Him every single concern. He will never leave you stranded.

Even in your hosting weaknesses, you can begin to invite others into your life and your home with confidence, knowing that the Lord will work in a wonderful way because He is God. That is what He does.

*Father, thank You for not leaving me all by myself. It's such a relief to know that I don't have to be strong all the time. You can and will use me for Your very good purposes when I trust You. Please be my strength when I have none. Work through my weaknesses for Your glory. In Jesus' name I pray, amen.*

## *Think It Over*

- What are some of your personal weaknesses? How have you watched the Lord work in your life despite these imperfections?
- How have you watched the Lord faithfully provide all that you've needed in the past by strengthening you in your weakness?
- What are your weaknesses and hesitancies when it comes to hosting?
- How have you watched the Lord give you enough strength in a hosting situation?
- How have you been able to welcome people through His strength and not your own?

## *Put It into Practice*

- It's time to step out in faith! Pray for guidance and courage. Invite someone to your home, even if it feels like a bit of a stretch. Watch and see how the Lord will work in your situation. Trust that He will give you the strength you need.

## *Home Work*

Does your home include a guest bedroom? If it does, you'll be working on this particular space for now. If you don't have a guest room, no worries! You'll think through where potential overnight guests could sleep. For starters, work on gathering sheets. Once the sheets for overnight guests have been collected, find cozy blankets and pillows for them to use. You're one step closer to welcoming them!

# The Struggle with Pleasing People

*Am I now trying to win the approval of human beings, or of God? Or am I trying to please people? If I were still trying to please people, I would not be a servant of Christ.*

Galatians 1:10

Depending on the people who surround you in your current season of life, the temptation and tendency to please people may be very strong.

People pleasing is nothing new. In fact, it's a powerful force that can motivate in positive or negative ways. If you're not firmly convinced regarding a specific matter, the persuasion and pressure from others can radically influence your thoughts and behaviors.

Peer pressure might shape your decisions about your values and opinions on current events, but it also can completely change your perspective and approach to hospitality. You might feel like your home should look a particular way or include certain accessories or renovations before you can invite others over. It's possible to struggle with accepting or appreciating your furnishings or feeling like you have to serve a particular kind of food or offer your guests a flawless experience before you offer any invitations.

That kind of invitation is centered on entertainment, though, and isn't necessarily considered hospitality. Why? Entertainment focuses on how you captivate, impress, amuse, or delight your guests. Entertaining others involves putting on a show. What could you serve and how could you best present your home to make the most spectacular impression?

While there's nothing wrong with delighting your guests, hospitality involves a kind and generous welcome that is sincere, pleasant, and friendly. Hospitality puts your guests first in a way that focuses on meeting their seen and unseen needs. Think of hospitality as more of a deep and genuine care for the people who enter your home as opposed to wowing your guests through entertainment.

While Paul didn't talk to the Galatian believers about hospitality, he did address pleasing people. At the beginning of his letter to the Galatian church, he clarified that he wasn't seeking the approval or pleasure of people. Instead, he wanted to please the Lord.

Boldly, Paul stated, "If I were still trying to please people, I would not be a servant of Christ." What a crystal-clear reminder that pleasing Christ usually looks very different from pleasing people. All throughout the New Testament, Christ's teachings typically seem like the polar opposite of what's accepted and embraced by the world.

What could all of this mean for your hospitality efforts? If you could welcome people into your life without trying to please them—but please and serve Christ instead—what would that look like?

Would your circle of friends become a lot more diverse, or would it stay the same? Would you begin to love others out of your love for and obedience to Christ instead of trying to seek anything in return?

If you began to live as a servant of Christ when you welcomed people into your home, who would receive your invitation?

As you begin to think more like Paul and choose to serve Christ instead of pleasing people, watch the way the Lord will change your heart, mind, and priorities. Watch the way He changes your choice and circle of companions. And watch the way He will transform you more and more into the likeness of Jesus.

*Father, it's refreshing to learn from Paul and know that serving Jesus is completely different from pleasing people. It was true for Paul, and it's even more relevant in today's world. Please help me realize every day that my choices reflect exactly whom I'm choosing to serve. Am I choosing Christ? Or am I choosing the world? I want to stay obedient to You. Please help me, even when it feels difficult. In Jesus' name I ask this, amen.*

## Think It Over

- Do you struggle with people-pleasing tendencies? When was peer pressure a driving force in your decision-making, either positively or negatively?
- What would your life look like if you focused on serving Christ instead of pleasing people?

- How many of your hosting experiences are centered on entertaining your guests? How much of a hospitality-centered mindset do you have?
- What simple changes could you make to focus more on your guests' needs instead of trying to impress them?

## *Put It into Practice*

- Plan a meal that's completely based on a mindset of hospitality. Who will you invite? How can you best minister to your guests? How can you ensure that you won't put a huge emphasis on what you'll serve or what your home will look like? If you struggle with overthinking or overplanning, inviting guests at the spur of the moment is a fun way to break your habit of entertaining.

## *Home Work*

Once you've gathered sheets, blankets and pillows, think about necessities that overnight guests would appreciate. How about an alarm clock and a small bedside lamp? Do you have some reading materials, earplugs, or a small fan or white noise machine? Think through what makes you feel nice and cozy and gather these homey touches for your guests. And if you don't have a guest room (but a pullout couch or air mattress), think of how you could incorporate cozy touches in a makeshift guest room.

# A Sacrifice That Pleases God

*Therefore, let us offer through Jesus a continual sacrifice of praise to God, proclaiming our allegiance to his name. And don't forget to do good and to share with those in need. These are the sacrifices that please God.*

Hebrews 13:15–16 NLT

When you hear the word *sacrifice*, what are the first thoughts that come to mind? Do you think of giving up something precious? Do you remember sacrifices other people made for you? Or sacrifices you made for others?

How many of your ideas and examples of sacrifice involve praise? Or doing good? Or sharing with people in need?

In Hebrews, it's explained that, through Jesus, continual sacrifices of praise to God demonstrate allegiance to the Lord. Additionally, doing good and sharing with those in need are sacrifices that please God.

Just as sacrifice involves surrendering something valuable for the sake of someone else, continual praise surrenders your attitude for the sake of the Lord. It involves finding reasons to praise even when you don't feel like it. Continually praising the Lord is a way to look for Him at work, even in less-than-desirable situations. And praising Him magnifies and exalts the Lord to His rightful place.

Along with your continual sacrifice of praise, another sacrifice that pleases the Lord is the sacrifice of good deeds. Mull that over for a moment. So often, good deeds can seem like favors that spring out of what *you'd* like to do. Feel like being generous today? You may suddenly be inspired to help someone, at your own convenience.

In the same mindset of "it's better to give than receive," it's easy to imagine that doing good to others will make both you and the other person feel better. However, if doing good is a sacrifice that pleases the Lord, knowing that it's a sacrificial good deed means that it comes at a cost to you.

In other words, you may not *feel* like doing a good deed. On the contrary, you may need to go out of your way or spend more money than you planned or feel inconvenienced in some way. That's okay. In fact, that's good. If you don't feel like doing good, yet you choose to do it anyway, you are making a sacrifice that brings joy to the Lord.

Similarly, sharing with others who are in need may seem inconvenient. Your generosity might come at a great cost for you, whether financially or with your time or effort. It might include opening your home or sharing a meal with someone. You may need to welcome someone you never intended. But choosing to give anyway is a wonderful gift. It's a worthy sacrifice. And it pleases the Lord.

As you make these sacrifices of praise and good deeds, know that it might *feel* like a sacrifice. But keep doing good and enjoy the good you receive as a result of your obedience and care for the Lord and others.

*Father, the sacrifice You desire is a broken spirit. You will not reject a broken and repentant heart, O God. I praise You for all You've done even in my brokenness. You still are God, no matter what happens in this world around me. You are awesome and holy. There is none like You, and I worship You. I offer my sacrifices of good deeds and generosity, even when I don't always feel like following through. Please let the words of my mouth, the meditations of my heart, and any goodness and generosity in my life be acceptable in Your sight, my Rock and Redeemer. In Jesus' name I pray, amen.*

## Think It Over

- When you consider all that typically seems like a sacrifice, do good deeds and acts of kindness come to mind right away? Why or why not?
- How often do you give the Lord a sacrifice of praise? What could you do to make this part of your day?
- How have people sacrificed for you through good deeds or help of some kind? Have you told them how much their generosity blessed you?
- How could your hospitality be a sacrifice that pleases the Lord?

## *Put It into Practice*

- Now's the perfect time to use your hospitality as a pleasing sacrifice to the Lord. Who could use the welcome of your home the most? How can you bless this person? Decide how and when you'll extend the welcome. Pray about the visit and consider how you can best honor the Lord through your hospitality. Then make an invitation and start the preparations!

## *Home Work*

To help any overnight guests feel at home, spend time putting together a welcome basket complete with a friendly note, Wi-Fi passwords, a bottle of water, and sample-size toiletries. You don't need to attempt to transform your home into a hotel, but think about nice touches that will make your guests feel at home.

# *Experiencing a Worry-Free Welcome*

*Don't worry about anything; instead, pray about everything. Tell God what you need, and thank him for all he has done. Then you will experience God's peace, which exceeds anything we can understand. His peace will guard your hearts and minds as you live in Christ Jesus.*

PHILIPPIANS 4:6–7 NLT

Do you consider yourself a worrier? When concerns pop up, do you worry and stew? Do you obsess and fret over details, whether real or imagined, until you work yourself into a tizzy? Or do you typically go with the flow and tend to experience peace instead of panic?

The fantastic reality of a life spent knowing, trusting, and resting in Christ is that He fills you and guards you with His peace. You don't have to worry. This freeing truth doesn't mean you can worry about less. It means you don't have to worry at all.

Instead, when you're feeling concerned, turn all of those concerns into prayers. Paul clearly explained this process to the church in Philippi: Instead of worrying, tell God what you need. Thank God for what He has done.

When you thank God, you'll be able to remember how He's faithfully worked and provided in the past. Moving past the mystery and uncertainty of what might happen to remember the reality and certainty of what *has* happened will take care of your worries in a hurry. Some of your memories may involve loss or pain, but they also should include the ways God provides and protects. He is the God who brings beauty from ashes, joy from mourning, and peace from despair (See Isaiah 61:3).

When you turn your worries into prayers, your prayers eventually turn to praise, and you'll experience God's indescribable and unexplainable peace. His unshakable peace, far greater than anything you can understand, guards your heart and your mind.

God's peace, experienced because of your prayers, is possible to have in the major trials of life. It's also available in everyday issues. Because the Lord truly wants to hear from you, nothing is too trivial for your prayers.

As you incorporate more praise and prayer into your everyday life, try praising Him for who He is and how He has worked, then honestly share what's on your mind. Tell Him how you feel and what you're thinking. Tell Him what you need and what you fear. Release these cares and concerns to Him, then truly trust Him to work.

This concept of trusting God with everything also includes your hospitality. As you open your life and your home to others more often, it can be tempting to try to do things in your own power and strength. From the way you care for your home to the menus you plan, the groceries you buy, and the preparations you make, it can be easy to forget about the Lord and get stressed or overwhelmed while you're in the middle of dealing with the details.

However, He's waiting for you to include Him. Talk with Him as you're thinking through ideas and making plans. As you clean and cook for your company, talk to Him about your preparations and the time together with others. Pray for the people who are coming to your home. Pray for your conversations. Pray that He'll multiply your preparation time and energy.

Keep praying and see how His supernatural peace will transform your heart and your mind. Pray, trust, and watch the Lord at work.

*Father God, You are so faithful and good to me. I truly don't have to worry about a single thing because You're in control. You work in wonderful ways. I want to share more of my life and my thoughts with You. Please help me know what You'd have me do. Please continue working in my life. Thank You for your peace, which is much bigger and greater than anything I can understand. Your peace through Jesus is absolutely amazing. In His name I pray, amen.*

## Think It Over

- How often do you try to take on all the cares of the world? How often do you try to deal with issues around the house on your own?
- How often do you come to the Lord with your concerns? How often do you talk with your heavenly Father about all that's on your mind, heart, and to-do list?
- How could His peace and help change your life?

## *Put It into Practice*

- The next time you're feeling overwhelmed with all you need to do around your home or the next time you try to figure out what to do when hosting someone, stop yourself and pray. Talk to the Lord and honestly share all that you're processing. Tell Him your concerns. Remember to thank Him for all He's done and for what He will do.

## *Home Work*

As a thoughtful touch for your overnight guests, make a list or welcome packet filled with ideas of what to see or do in your community. Any must-eat restaurants? Add them to the list. Shops or museums that are worth browsing? Write them down. Have fun thinking about your community with the wonder and wanderlust of a tourist.

# *Ministering Through Hospitality*

When you get busy with life, it's easy to focus on all that you need to do. It can be tempting to concentrate on your ever-growing to-do list. The same is true for hospitality. After you've invited guests to your home and you're in the middle of the preparations, it's so easy to get stuck concentrating on all of the details.

Yet hospitality and welcoming others include much more than to-do lists. There's an entire ministry of hospitality just waiting for your discovery. Part of this ministry begins with a proper focus. For whom are you working? And for whom are you welcoming? Are you doing all of the work and preparations just for your guests? Are you going to all the trouble of getting things just right for your own glory? Or are you welcoming guests for the Lord?

Once you clarify your motivation, it's time to consider your true purpose. You could welcome others as a way to encourage them or to help them through a difficult time. Maybe you simply want to get to know a new acquaintance better, or it's time to celebrate a special occasion. What if you began to see hospitality as a way to minister to other people. And what if you began to look at hospitality as a way to capture souls? Winning souls for Jesus just by opening your door and inviting people in could be a very powerful purpose to keep in mind.

As you make the mental shift from hospitality as simply a meal or an event to an investment in your guests' spiritual growth and eternity, you'll see how sacred the ministry of welcoming others can be.

# *From House to House*

*And every day, in the temple and from house to house, they did not cease teaching and preaching that the Christ is Jesus.*

Acts 5:42 esv

When you think about living out your faith each day, do you try to include a community of fellow believers? Do you intentionally try to stay connected with other Christ followers in everyday places?

For members of the early church, togetherness meant everything. Once Jesus died, rose from the dead, met and talked with hundreds of witnesses, then ascended into heaven, the early church exploded with growth. These men, women, and children knew the truth: Jesus was the Son of God. Some had watched His brutal death and witnessed that He was alive. Alive!

Christ's life after death changed everything. Suddenly, it didn't matter what humans said; these believing men and women were all in. They wanted to obey their risen Lord, and they wanted to spread the good news of Jesus everywhere and to everyone.

Because of this, the early church looked and behaved differently than many modern-day churches. Every day of the week, believers taught and preached that Jesus is the Christ. It didn't matter where this teaching and preaching happened. They taught in the temple, and they also taught from house to house.

As you consider creating and establishing a welcoming home, it's easy to associate hospitality with a welcome. And it's tempting to focus on temporal things, like where to sit with your guests or what kind of refreshments to serve. But what if you could use your home for so much more? What if you could use your home as a place where people learn that Jesus is the Christ? What if you could use your home to equip others to grow in their faith?

Of course, your home is a natural place to personally grow in your faith. A lot of prayer, praise, and Bible study can happen in your home. It's also an ideal place to disciple anyone who lives with you. But what if you began to intentionally use your home to reach others with the gospel? What if the welcoming atmosphere in your home is ideal for helping others grow in their relationship with Christ?

Truly, it doesn't matter where you live. If you've ever read about Corrie ten Boom's life, you know that Corrie and her sister Betsy were able to spread the gospel from the filthy confines of a concentration camp in the middle of World War II. Whether your home is a prison or a palace, the space where you live can be used to tell others about Jesus because you're there. You and your willingness are the keys.

While it's always tempting to think your home needs to look or feel a certain way before you can invite others in, *you* are the welcoming force. Not your stuff. And *you* are the one who can tell others about Jesus. *You* can help them grow in their faith and understanding.

As you welcome others into your home and life and truly live out your faith and beliefs in front of others, you will make a difference for Jesus. The things you say and do can help others understand that Jesus is the Christ.

Once this movement begins in your home and you invite others in, you never know how many other homes the truth will spread to, until the teaching of Jesus spreads from house to house, just like in the early church.

*Father, I'm grateful that so many men, women, and children in the early church not only came to know Jesus but also told others about Him. Because of their teaching and boldness, the Good News has been passed on for thousands of years! I want to follow their example. I want to tell others and teach others about the truth of Jesus. Please show me who I need to talk with, and please help me use my home in some way to make Your gospel truth known and understood. In Jesus' mighty name I pray, amen.*

## Think It Over

- How can you open up to better connect with other Christ followers?
- Who could you invite to your home to talk about Jesus?
- If you know someone who would like to learn more about Jesus and you're ready and willing to teach or learn with this person, consider meeting in your home for a Bible study, even if it's only two of you.

## *Put It into Practice*

- If you're ready to open your home as a place for others to get to know Jesus, look at your calendar. Which days of the week are better for you? Which times of the day would work well? Figure out your schedule, then start inviting!

## *Home Work*

One easy way to mentally prepare yourself for welcoming guests is to think through what you could serve them. Which of your meals receive the most compliments? What main dishes, side dishes, and desserts pair well? Are there any general themes that inspire you, like Italian, Mexican, or breakfast for dinner? How about soup in the winter or salad in the summer? What meal could be a crowd-pleaser? And what meal might suit picky eaters? What meals can you make with minimal stress? Make a list of potential company meals and keep it on hand for hosting opportunities.

# *Working for the Lord*

*Work willingly at whatever you do, as though you were working for the Lord rather than for people. Remember that the Lord will give you an inheritance as your reward, and that the Master you are serving is Christ.*

Colossians 3:23–24 NLT

How would you describe your hosting personality? What kind of a host are you? How might your guests describe your hospitality?

Your hospitality style is as unique as your personality. Depending on your personal tendencies, your hospitality efforts may be relaxed. You might feel comfortable opening your home at a moment's notice and welcoming others without any preparations. Going with the flow and offering whatever food you have around your house might work really well for you.

Or does the thought of an unannounced guest make you panic? Even with announced, planned guests, you might feel that hospitality adds a huge amount of work to your to-do list. Figuring out when to clean everything you'd like (along with planning, shopping, and preparing your food) might feel like a huge extra load that leaves you feeling frazzled.

Regardless of your comfort level with hospitality preparations, the reality is that welcoming extra people to your home always requires extra effort. But you also can expect to experience extra life with your company, in the way that welcoming different people into your home will add different views and conversations. Vibrancy will be added to your home in a way that simply wouldn't be there if you kept to yourself.

No matter how much or little work you feel you need to accomplish before welcoming people to your home, remember the vital truth of Colossians 3:23—work as though you're working for the Lord. Don't work like you're working for people. And as you labor for the Lord, do it willingly. Serve joyfully. Jump in and work with all your heart.

When you work in this way, you can forget about pleasing people. You don't have to concern yourself with picky details that might impress others for a moment but truly don't matter. Rather, you can choose larger aspects that glorify the Lord and wisely use His resources. You're not working for yourself or what you think your own hospitality efforts *should* be like. You don't even need to care if your attempts make you look good or not.

The bottom line is that you're serving Christ as you prepare for your guests. That means all the chores you do around your home, all the hospitality preparations you make, all the food you cook, and all the nooks and crannies you clean are done in service to Christ.

Instead of laboring for your own satisfaction or the praise of others, you'll end up with a reward from Christ for your hard work. He knows all you do when no one else is watching, and He'll reward you with an inheritance that's better than any earthly compensation.

Granted, all of your hard work is still work. And it is still hard. But it's not meaningless. It doesn't go unnoticed. Even if people don't mention a thing, the Lord knows what you've done to glorify and honor Him.

Keep doing the good work around your home and as you prepare to welcome guests. All of your efforts will bring a reward.

*Lord Jesus, I want to work for You. Remembering that all I do should bring You glory changes my perspective. It shapes my attitude. I may not always feel comfortable putting all of me into my work, but it does bring You glory. Please help me remember that You don't demand perfection. I also want to keep in mind that You sympathize with my weaknesses. Lead me to a healthy balance where I'm not obsessing over working harder than I should, but that I might work in a way that brings You glory. Give me strength to work hard, along with discernment to know my limitations. In Your name I pray, amen.*

## Think It Over

- What kind of a host are you: one who goes with the flow and isn't concerned with preparations? Or one who likes to plan, prepare, and make sure everything is just so?
- No matter how much attention to detail is important or not important to you, do you work for the Lord when you care for your home? Do you work with the Lord in mind when you prepare to host guests?

- Think about what life would look like if everything revolved around working for the Lord. What would stay the same? What would be different?

## *Put It into Practice*

- For the rest of today, do your household chores like you're working for the Lord. Tomorrow, try to do it again!

## *Home Work*

Once you've created a list of all the meals you'd like to serve your company, make master grocery lists for each one. (To make it handy, keep your list in your cell phone or email to access it when you're grocery shopping.) By having a list of all the ingredients you'll need, planning a dinner party or even simple appetizers or snacks will be quick and easy. Plus, you'll save yourself from making several trips to the store if you typically forget what you need to buy.

Devotion 42

# *Capturing Souls Through Hospitality*

*The fruit of the righteous is a tree of life, and whoever captures souls is wise.*

PROVERBS 11:30 ESV

When you think about hospitality, it can be tempting to limit your mindset to only inviting and hosting people in your home. You might plan the meal you'll cook, know what preparations you need to make so your home looks just so, or you might even take time to consider what kind of atmosphere you'd like to create. These kinds of hospitable ideas definitely can add to the overall experience when you host a guest, but, surprisingly, they don't need to remain the focus.

Instead of throwing all of your efforts into what your surroundings look like or what you'll offer your guests, step back and consider what they may really, truly *need*.

Depending on what's happening in life, your guests may need a listening ear or someone who can offer encouragement. They may need help processing all the details of a challenging situation. It might be helpful to take time together brainstorming possible next steps in life. If someone is weighed down with concerns, a good laugh might be amazing. And if a guest's everyday life is particularly busy, noisy, or stressful, offering a quiet, comfortable haven where he or she can decompress, relax, and feel refreshed would be wonderful.

Or your guest simply might need Jesus.

As a host, you get the privilege and responsibility not only of providing food, a place to relax, and a conversation but you also will need discernment to figure out what a guest truly needs. It's a tall order, if you're focusing on meal details or how comfortable your surroundings are while at the same time truly listening to your guest and figuring out how you can best help him or her. Knowing that there are much deeper issues while also tending to basic needs is important to remember. It's a juggling act that requires focus on what really matters.

Just like Proverbs 11:30 reveals, "Whoever captures souls is wise" (ESV). As you open your home—or if you're out and about and simply opening your life to others—use wisdom and discernment. Life is about so much more than polite conversations, good food, and comfortable places to meet. Bravely ask the difficult questions that will help your guest. Listen well and try to truly hear what's at the heart of your guest. Go out of your way to make your guest feel seen, heard, and known. In that knowing, don't be afraid to offer what truly matters. Instead of offering judgment, give grace. Rather than focusing only on the temporal, try to share the eternal. Using your wise discernment, ask the Lord to use your hospitality as a way to share the hope and truth of Jesus.

If you're wondering how or when to add some spiritual salt and light to your conversation, pray for an opportunity. Pray for your choice of words. Regardless of how comfortable or uncomfortable you may feel, you'll have a lot more credibility and persuasion talking about Jesus with someone who already knows you in some way. It could be as simple as sharing what Jesus has done in your life.

If you regularly host people you know and love, don't leave Jesus out of your conversations. Since He's part of your everyday life, He also can be part of your everyday discussions.

By trusting the Lord to guide your conversations, whether it's with people you're just getting to know or people you already know and love, the Lord can powerfully use your life stories, experiences, and hospitality. Pair your willingness to talk about what Jesus has done in your life with a welcoming attitude, and the Lord can and will use you in a mighty way.

*Lord, I am grateful You continue to welcome people to Your family. Thank You for always having room for one more. While it's been amazing to watch the way You've worked in my life, please help me be bold and caring enough to share these experiences with others around me. I want to tell others about all the good You've done in my life. Please use my hospitality to build your kingdom. I want to be welcoming so that I might be a part of winning souls to You. In Jesus' name I ask all of this, amen.*

## Think It Over

- What are some ways you've watched the Lord work in your life? How has He changed you? How can you tell people about these specific experiences?
- Among the people the Lord has brought into your life recently, which ones need to hear about what He's done for you? Who needs to hear your faith story?
- What are some ways you could use hospitality as an avenue to introduce others to Jesus?

## Put It into Practice

- Whether you feel like evangelism is your spiritual gift or you quake at the thought of talking to someone about Jesus, make it a point to start a spiritual conversation with one person this week. Watch how the Lord moves in your words.

## Home Work

If you'd like to become more intentional about inviting guests to your home, which hopefully is the case, it's wise to plan ahead. Make a list of snacks you'd like to offer unexpected company, from dried fruit, olives, and nuts, to cheese and crackers or special chocolates. Then little by little, create a stash of special groceries to share with company. Choose foods with long shelf lives, just in case you don't host company very often. To slowly build your stash, plan on buying one or two items a month. Now you'll always be ready for guests!

# *Known for Good Deeds*

*No widow may be put on the list of widows unless she is over sixty, has been faithful to her husband, and is well known for her good deeds, such as bringing up children, showing hospitality, washing the feet of the Lord's people, helping those in trouble and devoting herself to all kinds of good deeds.*

1 Timothy 5:9–10

What do you consider a good deed? Is it something you do to benefit other people? Or animals? Or nature? Do you do good as a way to improve an organization or agenda or church?

Good deeds can be almost anything. They're simply actions performed intentionally or consciously. They're something that you choose to do. And they are beneficial.

*Good* deeds stand out because of their merit. They're not bad or even average deeds. You consciously choose to do good.

The encouragement to do good is nothing new. In fact, good deeds have been emphasized for centuries. When Paul wrote to his disciple Timothy about how to lead churches, he specified what certain people should do and how certain people should be treated. For women—particularly widows—Paul listed qualities to emulate, including a devotion to good deeds.

What good qualities made it to the top of Paul's list? And what were some of the good deeds? A faithful marriage. Bringing up children. Washing the feet of the Lord's people—helping fellow believers in a humble, kind, and sacrificial way. Helping people who are in trouble. And showing hospitality. Each of those traits is good.

If you consider what all of those good deeds have in common, it's putting others first. Women known for good deeds put their own comfort aside to selflessly love others well. Even when you're tired, even when you don't feel like it—go out of your way to help others, whether it's your family members, believers, or other people who come and go from your life.

After Paul listed important family roles like wife and mother, what was next in his list of good deeds? Showing hospitality. Welcoming other people is a good deed.

As you welcome others into your home or your life, know that you are doing a good deed. Hospitality serves other people in a kind, selfless way. The opposite of opening your home in thoughtful hospitality is hoarding all of the comfort of your home, along with all of your kindness and compassion. You'd keep yourself hidden from the rest of the world, and, while you would be comfortable, cozy, and possibly content, other people in your sphere of influence would miss out on your goodness. Withholding hospitality from others would be withholding good from your corner of the world.

Choose to honor others through good works like hospitality. Choose to humbly serve other believers and help those in need. In doing so, you'll live out Christ's love in this weary world. Your goodness—and your hospitality—will make a difference for the better.

*Father, I want to be known for my good deeds as a way to show that I am Your follower. Please reveal to me my selfish habits that keep me from reaching out in generosity. Help me learn how to put others before myself. I want to show the love of Christ to those who need it most. Especially when it comes to hospitality, please open my eyes so I can see who needs my warm welcome. I want to invite people into my home as a way to share Your love generously and kindly. I pray that I will take Your opportunities as they come along. In Jesus' name I pray, amen.*

## Think It Over

- In your daily life, do you consider the good deeds you can do?
- Do you tend to think of others first? Do you seek to meet others' needs? Or do you spend most of your time and energy focusing on yourself?
- Looking at Paul's list of good deeds, what is one of your strengths? What's a weakness?
- Do you tend to consider hospitality as a good deed?

## *Put It into Practice*

- It's time to begin devoting yourself to good deeds! No matter what your living situation is, you can focus on serving other believers in humility, meeting the needs of the needy, and practicing hospitality.

## *Home Work*

Once you've created a plan for snacks to keep on hand for unexpected guests, it's time to select beverages you can keep on hand in case company comes calling. At the very least, stock up on flavorful tea bags so you could offer a cup of tea. Like your food items, buy one beverage a month. You'll keep expenses down but also establish a variety of offerings.

# *Waiting for Jesus with Anticipation*

*On the other side of the lake the crowds welcomed Jesus, because they had been waiting for him.*

Luke 8:40 NLT

How well do you wait? Do you tend to be a fairly patient person, or do you get frustrated whenever you're delayed?

When you know you're expecting company, do you rush around and stay busy until your guests arrive, or are you prepared far in advance? Do you sit down for a moment and enjoy the result of all your hard work? Or do you hurry and scurry until the doorbell rings? If your guests are delayed in arriving at your home or event, do you get frustrated, or are you relieved that you get extra time to prepare? Or do you get more and more excited with sheer anticipation?

During Jesus' earthly ministry, so many people wanted to have an in-person encounter with Him that they were willing to wait. Strangers flocked to Him once the word started to spread about the miracle-making Messiah. Whether they wanted to hear His teaching, receive His healing, experience the one-of-a-kind man who was God in the flesh, or they simply were curious, it was hard for Jesus to go anywhere without a crowd gathering.

Even when Jesus and His disciples would leave a community by boat, crowds still followed Him around the seashore. They waited and waited with anticipation, no matter how long Jesus and His disciples stayed in their boat. Even if members of the crowd felt impatient, it didn't matter. As soon as Jesus and His disciples reached the shore, the waiting crowds welcomed Him.

This sort of public ministry sounds exhausting, yet Jesus didn't send the people away. He knew they had great needs—physical and spiritual—that only He could meet. As Jesus revealed at the house of Zacchaeus (as documented in Luke 19), "the Son of Man came to seek and to save the lost."

No matter the demands that were placed on Jesus, His mission and intent were clear: "The Son of Man did not come to be served, but to serve, and to give His life as a ransom for many" (Mark 10:45). As He knew His purpose was to seek and to save, to serve and to give, Jesus perpetually poured Himself out in love. Everything He said and did centered on His purpose. His days and nights might have been full of people, but they also were full of purpose.

You might have come to know Jesus because someone chose to pour himself or herself out in an attempt to seek and save the lost. Maybe, as you were waiting, someone made the choice to serve you, and, as a result, you drew closer to Christ.

Perhaps you've decided to give your life away in order to serve others for Christ. If so, you'll face tiredness. You'll continually meet people who are waiting and in desperate need of the Lord's saving grace. The work and the service won't end.

But it's good work. You're willingly offering effort and service that will bring about eternal differences and eternal rewards. You'll live a life focused on helping others find and understand the welcome that only Jesus offers.

*Lord Jesus, it's an enormous blessing and undeserved gift that You came to seek and save the lost. You've rescued countless people for eternity. Thank You! Like You, I want to serve others as a way to point them to You and Your freedom. Please help me continue to labor for You, even when it's difficult, even when I'm tired. Please use me to bring others to Your kingdom. In Your name I pray, amen.*

## Think It Over

- Are you waiting to welcome Jesus into your life, like the crowds that waited on the seashore? Or are you figuratively in the boat with Jesus already, prepared to take His good news into the world?
- If you have a relationship with Christ, how are you sharing His welcome with people who don't know Him?
- If you're a Christ follower, are you following His mission to seek and save the lost? Are you taking time to serve others in His name? If not, why? What will you change to mirror His mission?

## *Put It into Practice*

- If you don't feel like you know Jesus, it's time to get to know Him. Start by reading the book of John in the New Testament. As you do, look for a local, Bible-believing, Bible-teaching church that can help you gain a better understanding of what it means to know Christ.
- If you do know Jesus, what is one way you can serve Him by serving other people? Identify this one way and do it. Don't delay. Get started working for Him.

## *Home Work*

Want a home project that will pack a punch? Focus on touches that will delight your guests. Make a playlist or two that would be perfect for company. Make sure you have enough coasters for hot or cold drinks. Can you think of anything else that would make your home particularly welcoming to guests? Maybe it's candles or an essential oil diffuser. Perhaps you need to stock up on extra light bulbs or dig out your coziest throw blanket. Whatever you need to gather, this is your prompt to do it!

## Section Eleven

# *Welcoming Through Unforgettable Events*

Every person is unique, and every event is unique. From the number of guests to where you meet and what you serve, no two events are alike. You may prefer more intimate gatherings over coffee or a quiet dinner. Not every event needs to be an all-out big bash, but it might still be remarkable.

From celebratory meals to holiday feasts, if you invite a large crowd, you can anticipate an unforgettable occasion. These special events require initiative to host. They also include plenty of details. What will you serve everyone? Where will you seat everyone? Who is coming?

Your willingness to plan and host an event may also include recognizing a guest of honor, whether it's the birthday boy, a recent graduate, or a loved one who's moving away. As you consider these special guests, pray that the Lord will use your gathering in a special way.

Consider, for a moment, family feasts and large theme parties of your past. Do you still remember certain details, from the outfit you wore to where you sat? Now think about simple family meals from your childhood. You had many more daily meals, but chances are they blend together in your mind.

Special events stick out because they're out of the ordinary. As you plan special events, you'll need to take the initiative. You'll also need to address logistical realities, no matter how challenging they might seem.

As you plan and prepare, remember that you're creating a special atmosphere. To avoid adding pressure, don't worry about planning the biggest and the best. Rather, remember that by taking the time to prepare an occasion, you're helping to create unforgettable memories for your guests.

# *Taking the Initiative to Host*

*One day Elisha went to Shunem. And a well-to-do woman was there, who urged him to stay for a meal. So whenever he came by, he stopped there to eat. She said to her husband, "I know that this man who often comes our way is a holy man of God. Let's make a small room on the roof and put in it a bed and a table, a chair and a lamp for him. Then he can stay there whenever he comes to us."*

2 Kings 4:8–10

Women can be very persuasive, especially when they set their minds to accomplishing something specific. From rallying support for a particular cause to organizing efforts to care for others in need, women have been change-makers throughout history.

The prophet Elisha benefited greatly from the determination, hospitality, and persistent persuasion of a Shunammite woman.

However Elisha and the Shunammite woman met, one thing's for certain: She knew he was a holy man of God. Elisha felt comfortable enough to return to the woman's home whenever he was in Shunem. After getting to know him, this hospitable, well-to-do woman suggested to her husband that they add a guest room for Elisha to their home.

It wasn't just any guest room. This hostess with the mostess planned to furnish the rooftop room with a bed, table, chair, and lamp, which seems pretty impressive for Old Testament times. Plus, this room was Elisha's very own place so he could come, eat, and rest whenever he was in the area, which was ideal for this hard-working traveling prophet.

Today, we can learn several fantastic lessons from the Shunammite woman. For starters, when you have a heart for hosting others, don't be afraid to make an invitation. Elisha didn't ask for a meal. And he didn't ask for a place to stay. The well-to-do woman from Shunem took the initiative. While he was enjoying his meal, she must have welcomed him, made him feel comfortable, and invited him to come back, because he continued to stop at her home to eat while passing through Shunem, even before she initiated the guest room idea.

Another important lesson we can learn is to pay attention to what people need the most. Keep your eyes and ears open for possibilities. Once you recognize a need, find a solution. Not only did the Shunammite woman know that Elisha needed a good home-cooked meal but she also noticed that he needed a place to stay. Instead of sending him on his way hungry and homeless, she told her husband they'd create a space for this special visitor. She didn't wait for Elisha to verbalize his needs. She didn't stall so someone else could create a solution. She got to work and used her family's resources to bless Elisha in amazing, generous ways.

Similarly, when you notice someone is in need, it's kind to proactively spring into action. Use resources like your home, your food, and your finances to bless other people, even if they don't ask for help or mention their need. Taking initiative brings a huge blessing to people's lives without making them feel like they must ask for what they desperately need.

*Father God, thank You for the good example from the woman in Shunem. Please help me to be more like her and show initiative when it comes to inviting and hosting others. I want to be welcoming! Please help me be generous and kind to others. Sometimes I get so wrapped up in my own world that it's difficult to spy the needs of others. Please help me be perceptive. Most of all, I want to be proactive and find others I can help, all for Your glory. In Jesus' name I ask this, amen.*

## Think It Over

- Have you met someone who clearly needed a little help, whether with practical, physical needs like meals, clothing, a place to stay, or finances? Have you met someone who had deeper needs that required professional help? In either case, what did you do?
- Have you experienced the unexpected gift of someone else's hospitality when you needed it most? What happened?
- What kind of space does your home have for overnight guests? Just like the Shunammite woman planned how to furnish her guest space, what furniture and hospitality essentials could you use?

- When you recognize a man or woman of God, how can you show honor and kindness?

## *Put It into Practice*

- Like the woman in Shunem, be on the lookout for people's unspoken needs. Help someone in a very practical way without being asked.
- Invite someone for dinner. This person might live down the street but would still appreciate a shared meal.

## *Home Work*

If you host a feast, you're choosing to host a very special occasion. Even when you have a relaxed attitude toward hospitality, a lot of elements come into play here. To make the process easier, begin by creating a menu. Exactly what do you plan to serve? What can other people bring? Once you've created your initial menu, think through the logistics. Have you planned too much food? Too many options? Will you have enough food or variety for everyone? Think about this for a day or two, then revisit and revise your ideas.

# Miraculous Multiplication Can Feed a Multitude

*That evening the disciples came to him and said, "This is a remote place, and it's already getting late. Send the crowds away so they can go to the villages and buy food for themselves." But Jesus said, "That isn't necessary—you feed them." "But we have only five loaves of bread and two fish!' they answered." "Bring them here," he said. Then he told the people to sit down on the grass. Jesus took the five loaves and two fish, looked up toward heaven, and blessed them. Then, breaking the loaves into pieces, he gave the bread to the disciples, who distributed it to the people. They all ate as much as they wanted, and afterward, the disciples picked up twelve baskets of leftovers. About 5,000 men were fed that day, in addition to all the women and children!*

MATTHEW 14:15–21 NLT

If you've ever hosted a large group of people, you know how difficult it can be to assess how much food you need to serve. If you underestimate, people might leave hungry. If you overestimate, you have leftovers for days. Calculating the Goldilocks factor—not too little, not too much, but just right—is really difficult. Plenty of other obstacles can crop up, too, like issues with your budget, space, time, or energy to prepare or serve.

The disciples needed to serve many people with a seemingly impossible amount of food. Throughout their time with the Son of God, these disciples witnessed countless miracles. Over and over, they had experienced the impossible made possible through the Messiah. Yet over and over, despite the miraculous, the disciples still found themselves sidetracked and distracted by ordinary challenges.

When Jesus asked them to feed a crowd of more than five thousand, the disciples focused on their limitations. How, in the middle of nowhere, could they serve thousands of people? The only food they had were five loaves of bread and two fish.

Like the disciples, when Jesus provides opportunities for us to serve and feed people, it can feel daunting, especially if there are obvious limitations. How can you feed a crowd if you don't have much room? How can you feed guests when finances are tight?

It can be tempting to focus on what seems impossible, just as the disciples did. Yet just like the disciples, you follow and serve the God of impossibilities. Jesus multiplied the humble offering of two fish and five loaves of bread, and He can multiply details in your life. Have you asked for His help?

The next time you know you need to serve or welcome or feed others and you don't have the capacity to do so, pray. Thank the Lord for this opportunity to trust Him. Thank Him for all of His blessings. Then ask Him to do the miraculous. Ask Him to multiply your time and energy. Ask Him to provide food or room. Ask Him to help people feel welcomed and loved. Then trust that He will do the miraculous, because He will. It may look nothing like you expect, but He will work. He's the God of miraculous multiplication.

*Lord Jesus, You are the Son of God. All things are possible with You. I pray that I remember this and trust You with all of my concerns, big or small. When it comes to trusting You for Your provision, may I never doubt You. You can and will provide all I need, according to Your riches in glory. As I love and serve other people as a way to glorify You, please multiply everything I need, whether it's resources (like money, food, or space), or something deeper like my energy or love and compassion. You are the God of miracles, and I can't wait to watch You work in me and through me. In Your name I pray, amen.*

## Think It Over

- Are you easily sidetracked and distracted by ordinary challenges? How can you use prayer to combat this tendency?
- When have you watched the Lord provide for you in a miraculous way? Did His provision look like anything you imagined?
- When it comes to serving others, what is one of your typical limitations? Do you feel exhausted and out of energy? Are your finances drained? Do you have enough help from others? Do you have enough space?
- Have you ever watched your limitations become strengths?

## *Put It into Practice*

- Consider the challenges you just thought about. You know your limitations better than anyone else. Now that you've thought about what seems to be impossible, it's time to give it all to the Lord. Pray a bold prayer of trust and reliance on Him. Instead of holding on to any doubt or fear, surrender it to Him. Ask Him to help your unbelief and ask Him to provide.

## *Home Work*

Once you've thought through a menu for your special event, holiday, or feast, it's time to start planning the logistics. (While this may seem like a lot of work on the front end, you'll be grateful as your big event gets closer.) Start working through the details by finding all the recipes for your meal. Try any new recipes ahead of time, just to make sure they taste great. Once you've finalized your menu and tracked down your recipes, create a grocery list. Now you'll be ready to go shopping once your dinner date gets closer!

# Hosting a Meal of Honor

*Six days before the Passover, Jesus came to Bethany, where Lazarus lived, whom Jesus had raised from the dead. Here a dinner was given in Jesus' honor. Martha served, while Lazarus was among those reclining at the table with him.*

John 12:1–2

How do you repay someone who has given you the most amazing, generous gift you've ever received? How do you let the giver know that you're truly thankful? In the gospel of John, we get a glimpse of one amazing gift and a fantastic display of gratitude.

Remember the account of Jesus visiting the sisters Mary and Martha in Luke 10:38–42? Martha was busy preparing for her guests while Mary sat listening to Jesus. When Martha was upset by Mary's lack of help, she approached Jesus with her complaint: "Lord, don't you care that my sister has left me to do the work by myself? Tell her to help me!"

"'Martha, Martha,' the Lord answered, 'you are worried and upset about many things, but few things are needed—or indeed only one. Mary has chosen what is better, and it will not be taken away from her.'"

Often, Martha gets a bad reputation for focusing on the work required for her hospitality. But in John chapter 12, you can get another peek into Martha's hospitality, and it's a wonderful thing.

Lazarus, Martha's brother, was dead and buried for four days before Jesus came and restored life to His dead friend. By this point in their friendship, Martha and Jesus clearly were comfortable enough with each other to have frank conversations. Just as Jesus talked to Martha about her focus in His earlier visit, Martha wasn't afraid to tell Jesus that Lazarus would have lived if Jesus had been there.

Martha also was certain who Jesus was: "I believe that you are the Messiah, the Son of God, who is to come into the world" (John 11:27).

After Jesus brought Lazarus back to life, Martha wanted to thank her friend Jesus. But what could she do? How could she show her unspeakable gratitude for bringing her brother from death to life?

Martha did something she knew she could do with excellence: She opened her home and invited others to attend a dinner in Jesus' honor. Can you imagine the feast to thank the Messiah for bringing her brother back from the dead? Can you imagine the welcome she gave Jesus and His disciples?

Martha set a fantastic example anyone can imitate. If you receive an unbelievable gift of great worth, or you receive something you could never repay, a thoughtful and effective way to show your gratitude is through hospitality. Invite the giver into your home. Warmly welcome and show your thankfulness by a meal. Invite others, if you wish, to truly make the evening a celebration.

Hosting a meal to honor someone and then diving right in to serve your guest of honor is a priceless and truly meaningful way to say thank you.

*Lord Jesus, just like Martha, I believe that You are the Messiah, the Son of God. You deserve all the honor and glory and praise. Thank You for the miracles, seen and unseen, You perform in my life. Please open my eyes to see the situations and people that deserve my honor and thankfulness. When I spy them, help me work out all the details so I can show honor through my hospitality. In Your name I pray, amen.*

## Think It Over

- When have you received an over-the-top, priceless gift that could never be repaid? How did you express your thankfulness?
- Why do you think hosting a dinner in someone's honor is so meaningful?
- Imagine wanting to show your gratitude with a meal. What could you do to make this event extra special? What could you serve? How could you respect and esteem your guest of honor?

## Put It into Practice

- Who do you need to thank right now? Can you think of anyone who needs to experience your gratitude with a meal? If so, it's time to make an invitation!

## *Home Work*

If your special event or feast is approaching quickly, it's time to put your plans in motion. By now you know what you'd like to serve. You know what you need to buy. The next step, before you start cooking, is figuring out how much time your food preparation should take, as well as how long everything needs to cook. When does your food need to go in the oven? What can you prepare first? What needs to wait until right before mealtime? The more complex your meal, the more preparation and cooking time you'll need. Even if you need two or more days to prepare food, figure out your plan and write it out. When the day finally arrives, stick to your plans, cook according to your schedule, and enjoy a meal without quite so much stress.

# Satisfied by an Abundance

*Jesus called his disciples to him and said, "I have compassion for these people; they have already been with me three days and have nothing to eat. I do not want to send them away hungry, or they may collapse on the way." His disciples answered, "Where could we get enough bread in this remote place to feed such a crowd?" "How many loaves do you have?" Jesus asked. "Seven," they replied, "and a few small fish." He told the crowd to sit down on the ground. Then he took the seven loaves and the fish, and when he had given thanks, he broke them and gave them to the disciples, and they in turn to the people. They all ate and were satisfied. Afterward the disciples picked up seven basketfuls of broken pieces that were left over. The number of those who ate was four thousand men, besides women and children.*

Matthew 15:32–38

So often in life, it's easy to get distracted by everyday stresses and shortcomings. Focusing on the urgent and immediate makes it hard to step back and turn to the Lord for His strength. It's tempting to doubt God's provision without even asking Him about it in prayer.

After Jesus fed the five thousand in Israel, He kept moving along with His disciples, teaching and healing more and more people. When they traveled close to the Sea of Galilee, "Great crowds came to Him, bringing the lame, the blind, the crippled, the mute and many others, and laid them at His feet; and He healed them" (Matt. 15:30).

Even after all the ways He ministered to the crowds of people for days, Jesus had never-ending compassion for them. He knew their needs and their wants. He knew they were spiritually hungry, and physically hungry. And He knew that He could satisfy both hungers.

At that moment, He was ready to give the hungry crowds food. Again, His disciples wondered how they could feed the vast crowds on their own, and again Jesus was ready to multiply the little bits of food that were available.

Just like when He fed the 5,000, Jesus thanked the Lord for the food. Then

He broke the loaves of bread and fish to give to the disciples, who passed around enough food to feed more than 4,000 men, women, and children.

The people ate until they all were satisfied. In fact, by the time everyone had finished eating, there were leftovers to spare.

Sometimes you'll invite people into your home and not know how you can provide for everyone. You may not even know what you can possibly serve your family for dinner. Jesus miraculously provided for those who crowded to hear His teaching, and He will provide for you.

Follow Jesus' example and begin by gathering your food. Give thanks to the Lord for His provision. After you've prayed, divide the food among those you're feeding. No matter the size of your crowd, show compassion by welcoming and feeding, all while trusting His provision. Watch the way He provides until all are satisfied!

*Lord God Almighty, You provide all things. Why do I ever concern myself with wondering if You will? Nothing is impossible for you. Nothing is beyond You or Your power and might. Nothing surprises You. I want to live with this certainty. When I'm tempted to doubt or dwell on what seems impossible, please remind me to trust You in faith. I don't want to be limited to believing in only what I can see. I fully believe You are before all things and in You all things hold together. I want to rest in this complete trust of You! In Jesus' name I pray, amen.*

## Think It Over

- When you face a seemingly impossible situation, how often do you fret about details and impossibilities? How often do you stop to turn your worries over to the Lord and trust Him to provide?
- When has the Lord provided or stretched food for you in an amazing way? What did you feel like before, during, and after this experience?
- In what unique ways or situations have you watched God provide food or other necessities for you or others?
- How often do you find yourself stepping out in faith, trusting the Lord to fully provide?

## *Put It into Practice*

- The next time you're in a needy situation, stop yourself from worrying or dwelling about details. Instead, make a conscious choice to pray about your specific need. As you pray, thank God in advance for His perfect provision. When worries crop up again, pray more. Repeat the process until you truly rest in your trust of your heavenly Father.

## *Home Work*

All of your preparation for your guests should be complete. You're ready to host a great gathering! The last thing to do should be part of every step of your preparation process: pray! Pray for the Lord to be glorified in your hospitality attempts. Pray for conversations. Pray for your guests to feel welcomed and honored. Pray that you'll all enjoy your time together. Whatever else comes to mind, pray about it. Lift up your time as a host in prayer. When you're working through your plans and are busy cleaning or cooking, pray. Ask the Lord to work through your efforts and do it all to glorify Him.

# *Blessing Others and Yourself with Hospitality*

Hospitality is a wonderful way to blend your creativity, thoughtfulness, and kindness in a tangible way that blesses your guests. Instead of wondering how someone could feel blessed, you have an opportunity to actually follow through and do it in your own home.

While certain aspects are nice, hospitality can include so much more than a warm welcome, a meal, a good conversation, and a place to sit and rest. You can use your hospitality as a way to draw your guests to Christ.

Jesus is ready to welcome all who believe in Him to His kingdom. Following His lead and example, we can do the good work of telling people about Him. If the only way to His kingdom is to first hear about Him, then we need to proactively tell others about Jesus. Opening our homes to others helps us offer comfortable and safe spaces to grow spiritually. So many healthy, helpful discussions can take place outside of church buildings—in the spaces we spend each day.

Fortunately, God's Word offers many ways to create a righteous focus in your life and home. As we continue to use our homes and hospitality with a specific spiritual center, we'll receive blessings here on earth. One day we'll also be welcomed into our eternal home and (hopefully) realize that many guests who graced our earthly homes are there too.

# *Imitating the Welcome of Christ*

*May the God of endurance and encouragement grant you to live in such harmony with one another, in accord with Christ Jesus, that together you may with one voice glorify the God and Father of our Lord Jesus Christ. Therefore welcome one another as Christ has welcomed you, for the glory of God.*

Romans 15:5–7 esv

So much of life is learned by observing and imitating other people. In every family, children copy what is modeled to them. For generations, apprentices watched and followed the ways of journeymen, then master craftsmen, as they learned, honed, and perfected their crafts. For Christians, a powerful aspect of discipleship is for a younger believer to observe and mirror the attitudes, traits, and faithful life of an older, seasoned believer.

Yet if there's anyone worth imitating, it's Jesus. His unconditional, sacrificial love and way of life is what His believers need to emulate. While there are countless ways to model your life after Christ's, Paul gave Roman believers a very direct charge: Welcome each other, as Christ welcomed you.

Much like Paul's command to forgive one another, "as God in Christ forgave you" (Eph. 4:32 esv), this command is similar. Do to others what Christ already did for you.

When you think of becoming more like Christ, welcoming other people may not be the first thing that comes to mind. Yet welcoming makes perfect sense. Once you choose Jesus as your Lord, you experience Christ's welcome into His family. (To be clear, choosing Jesus Christ as your Lord and Savior is as simple as confessing with your mouth that Jesus is Lord and believing in your heart that God raised Him from the dead, as explained in Romans 10:9.) When He welcomes you, you're no longer an outsider. You're no longer separated from Him. Nothing can separate you from His love.

If this is true of your life and eternity, it's time for your choices, behaviors, and habits to change. One way you should be affected (for the better!)

is to begin welcoming others into your life, home, and surroundings, just like Christ has welcomed you.

Depending on your personality, this might be incredibly easy, or it might feel pretty awkward or even painful at first. Regardless of how you feel, it's important to be welcoming. Be kind. Be thoughtful. Consider how others might want to be welcomed, and then follow through and do it.

As you start welcoming others into your life, sometimes you'll experience joy when your efforts go smoothly. The scheduling might work out perfectly. All of your food preparation may be spot-on. Welcoming new people can feel like a huge success when you realize you have a lot in common and really enjoy each other's company.

But at other times, you'll experience frustrations when your hosting or welcoming doesn't go according to your plans or hopes. In fact, some moments might feel like absolute disasters.

Have you gone out of your way to invite someone who declined your invitation? Were you ready to welcome someone new into your home, only to discover a maintenance catastrophe had hit your home? Have you ever made a bunch of plans and preparations, only to have the weather or health issues or life situations force you to reschedule or cancel? Do you welcome people into your life, only to find out they're argumentative and critical?

While you certainly can't ensure the outcome of your welcoming efforts, you can rest in the fact that you're trying to glorify God. As Paul reminds in Romans 15:5, God is the God of endurance and encouragement. He can help you endure even the trickiest, stickiest situations. He can bring encouragement as you enjoy hospitality victories. And through it all, whether your attempts are successes or failures, He is the one who can help you live—and welcome others—in harmony.

However your welcoming attempts are received, remember that when you welcome others, you're welcoming them to glorify the God and Father of our Lord Jesus Christ. Just as Christ welcomed you into His family when you were an outsider, welcome others. Just as Christ will welcome believers into His home one day, welcome others into your home now.

Every time you choose to welcome others, you're choosing to live in harmony that's granted from God. He gives you the grace and love and words to say when you're hosting people you don't know very well. And He blesses the conversations and strengthens relationships when you're hosting people you do know well.

As you welcome others for God's glory, you prove that you've not only observed the way Christ has welcomed you but you've also emulated His welcome. Like a good apprentice or disciple, you're trying to be more and more like Him. And that choice glorifies God.

*Father, thank You so much for welcoming me into Your family through Jesus Christ. Your welcome has changed absolutely everything in my life and my future. Please help me show Your loving and kind welcome to people I meet and people I need to get to know better. Please give me the courage to smile and be a welcoming person, whether it's simply through conversations or something deeper, like inviting people into my home and life. Through it all, however You stretch me, I want to glorify You. In Jesus' name I pray, amen.*

## Think It Over

- How have you been welcomed by Christ? What about Christ's welcome frees you up to welcome others, both relationally and into your home?
- When it comes to inviting others into your life, what, if anything, do you think is standing in your way? How can you best hand this over to the Lord and trust Him to change you to become more welcoming?
- Do you feel like you need the Lord's endurance and encouragement as you consider welcoming others into your life?
- Are you naturally a person who strives for harmony with others, or are harmonious relationships a struggle for you?
- Do you already welcome others into your life like Christ has welcomed you? Or is a Christ-like, welcoming attitude something you need to ask for and trust Him to change in your heart?

## Put It into Practice

- It's time to trust the Lord for endurance! No matter what season of life you're in, as you focus on becoming more welcoming, you'll need endurance when challenges or potential excuses arise.

- Once you know *whom* you should welcome, it's time to get busy! What's one easy, non-threatening way to show someone that you care? What's a kind way to welcome this person?
- As you acclimate yourself to becoming more welcoming, make sure you're doing it all for the Lord's glory and not your own. Don't forget to examine your motives.

## Home Work

Not all of your hospitality needs to happen within the four walls of your home. You may want to invite a friend, family member, or new acquaintance to meet you somewhere out and about. If you choose to host a get-together outside of your home (whether it's literally outside your home on your front porch, back patio, or somewhere else) or at a park or other public place, you still need to prepare. Gather paper products ahead of time for your on-the-go hosting opportunities. If you keep everything in a handy bag, basket, or box, you can take your disposable supplies with you whenever hosting inspiration strikes!

# *Blessings Even in the Presence of Enemies*

*You prepare a feast for me in the presence of my enemies. You honor me by anointing my head with oil. My cup overflows with blessings. Surely your goodness and unfailing love will pursue me all the days of my life, and I will live in the house of the* LORD *forever.*

PSALM 23:5–6 NLT

Imagine sitting down to a sumptuous feast. You're ready to (politely) dig into everything set before you when you notice your enemies are in the other room, observing all the preparations. Feel a little awkward? Sit back, say grace, and help yourself to the food and drink. This meal is in your honor, and you are invited to enjoy it.

While this seems like an unlikely scenario, it's a wonderful picture of the life of a believer. David knew, as he penned the poetry of Psalm 23, what it was like to go through life with enemies. He knew what it was like to experience the way God poured out immense blessings even when his foes watched and threatened him with danger at every turn.

No matter what David faced, he knew the Lord planned and prepared blessings regardless of who was in his life. He knew the Lord anointed him to his position. Because of the Lord's goodness and unfailing love, David knew he had been blessed abundantly. He could reflect on the moments of his life and remember how the Lord's love and goodness pursued him.

Like David, spend time reflecting on your life. How has God pursued you with His goodness? How has His unfailing love chased after you? How has the Lord honored you? Has He anointed you and placed you in a special position? In what ways has the Lord showered His blessings on you, even with your enemies looking on?

While Psalm 23 is brimming with spiritual implications, consider its practical aspects. When you host guests, do you ever need to invite people who are at odds with each other? If so, you know how uncomfortable it can be as you hope and pray that everyone will get along. Disagreements are part of life and part of relationships—some more than others. Instead of avoiding conflicts at all costs, peacemakers attempt to bring opposing sides together. Much like the Lord prepares feasts for His beloved in the presence of enemies, sometimes you'll prepare meals or welcome people who would rather not be in the same room with each other.

When these sticky situations arise, follow the truth of Psalm 34:14—Seek peace and pursue it. In His Sermon on the Mount, Jesus taught that peacemakers are blessed and will be called children of God.

As a child of God, it's not enough to quietly sit by in peace. Avoiding conflict doesn't establish peace. Rather, walking into less-than-desirable situations to attempt to smooth over conflicts between two opposing sides makes peace. If coworkers are at odds with each other, children or siblings are fighting, or people in your neighborhood take sides against each other, work for peace. Even if it means inviting people over to try to mend fences around your dinner table, prepare a feast and set the tone for some peace-filled conflict resolution.

This determination to encourage peace and resolve conflict isn't easy, but it's vital. And this kind of peace-making hospitality has the potential to change lives and future relationships.

*Father, You are so good to bless me. It doesn't even matter who's around. I might be surrounded by my friends or enemies, but You'll still pour out Your blessings on me, because that's the kind of good God You are. Thank You for Your goodness. Thank You for loving me with a never-ending, never-failing love. I pray I won't squander all Your blessings on myself, and I don't want to take them for granted. Please help me mimic You and Your goodness and love. Help me be kind to others. Use me as a peacemaker even in situations that feel uncomfortable. I want to be used by You in the lives of others. In Jesus' name I pray, amen.*

## Think It Over

- When and how did God invite you to His feast so that you could live in His house forever? When did you accept His invitation?

- Have you watched the Lord pour out His blessings on you, even in the presence of your enemies?
- How have His unfailing love and goodness pursued you today?
- Who could use your peaceful presence? Could you be a peacemaker in that person's life?

## *Put It into Practice*

- Decide to face conflict head-on. Instead of avoiding awkward situations, do the difficult but necessary job of a peacemaker. Decide how you can use your home to encourage peaceful resolution for others.

## *Home Work*

If you have a great space for outdoor hosting, whether it's on a balcony, breezeway, porch, patio, or deck, assemble a kit that's fit for outdoor hosting. When you're in the middle of outdoor dining, what will you need the most? Collect paper napkins or paper towels, silverware, plates, cups, and serving dishes that will withstand outdoor elements, along with candles or other decorations. Once you've gathered everything, keep it in one spot, close to your outdoor space, making outdoor entertaining very easy and low-key.

# Storing Up Your Treasure

*Do not store up for yourselves treasures on earth, where moths and vermin destroy, and where thieves break in and steal. But store up for yourselves treasures in heaven, where moths and vermin do not destroy, and where thieves do not break in and steal.*

MATTHEW 6:19–20

Turn on any device and observe the messages you're receiving, whether it's on a TV, the internet, or your emails and texts. How long does it take until you're bombarded with messages about things you "need" to purchase?

Whether you're encouraged to make "lasting" purchases—like homes, vehicles, furnishing, electronics, clothing, or jewelry—or fleeting purchases—like food, travel, cosmetics, or health products—one thing is absolutely certain: None of those "treasures" will truly last. Every one of those purchases has the potential to break or get stolen or become outdated and obsolete.

Advertisers and influencers hawk their goods in hopes of making a sale, but their products won't last. They're temporal. And truly, in the big scope of life, they're meaningless.

If all earthly stuff is fleeting, what does last? As the Gospels Matthew, Mark, and Luke record, Jesus taught, "Heaven and earth will pass away, but my words will never pass away," (Matt. 24:35, Mark 13:31, and Luke 21:33). Human souls will also last forever. As Jesus taught in Matthew 10:28, "Do not be afraid of those who kill the body but cannot kill the soul. Rather, be afraid of the One who can destroy both soul and body in hell."

Accepting the truth that our belongings will not last but the Word of God and souls do last, it's possible to figure out what is worth spending your time focusing on while you're here on earth.

Jesus taught that you can store up your treasures in heaven. You can start by intentionally spending time in the Word and building into others in a spiritual sense. It might involve a radical life change, or it might start with taking your eyes off of yourself and your own comfort and looking to the needs of others.

One way to bring this process close to home—or actually *into* your home—is by welcoming others with the intent of pointing them to Christ. Whether this welcome takes place around your kitchen table or in the hallways of your church or even at a local park or coffee shop, remember that you can invest your time, energy, and finances in something that lasts forever. You can choose to forget about focusing on the things of this world.

As you change your focus, you may discover the gift of using your home in hospitality. So often, it's easy to think you have to go far away to reach the unreached for Christ. It's tempting to consider that if you fly halfway around the globe, maybe you could make a difference for eternity. Yet look exactly where you are! God has placed you right here in this place, at this moment in history, for a specific purpose. You have the luxury of using your own surroundings, where, hopefully, you're the most comfortable and at ease, to minister to other people. You can use your heartfelt welcome and intentional hospitality to help others discover the Lord.

Take the opportunities He brings to you, wherever you are, and use them wisely. Be grateful that a ministry for Him can start simply, with a welcome to others in your life.

*Father God, You have such a perfect plan. It's freeing to know that You intended for certain things to remain forever. Please help me focus on these forever things. I want to know and love Your Word more and more every day. I also want to remember that I can make an impact in the lives of other people—and this impact can last for eternity. It's tempting to get sidetracked and distracted by the stuff of earth. Please help me to keep my focus on You and to move past all the fun but fleeting pleasures that truly don't matter. I want to stay devoted to You and Your good work for my life. In Jesus' name I pray, amen.*

## Think It Over

- Which earthly treasures are sapping your energy and time? How have you watched these items begin to age and wear out?
- How do you focus on storing up treasures in heaven? What helps you keep this focal point?
- How can you use your home as a place to reach others for Christ?

- What specific ways can you use this particular time in history and the place where God has directed you to begin or continue storing up heavenly treasures?

## *Put It into Practice*

- Once you've considered ways to use your home to store up treasures in heaven, put one of these ideas into practice. Choose one of your ideas. Think through practical details and make this possibility a reality!

## *Home Work*

Once you've gathered everything you need for outdoor, on-the-go entertaining (from seating to plates, cups, and paper products), create a manageable plan. Exactly how do you plan to set everything up? How do you plan to clean everything up? Figure out what you may need, from the time that everything may take, to small details like keeping garbage bags on hand so you can throw away paper plates or cups. Don't forget insect repellent, charcoal for grilling, and any other detail that would make your outdoor event easier for you and enjoyable for everyone.

# A Rich Welcome into Eternity

*His divine power has given us everything we need for a godly life through our knowledge of him who called us by his own glory and goodness. Through these he has given us his very great and precious promises, so that through them you may participate in the divine nature, having escaped the corruption in the world caused by evil desires. For this very reason, make every effort to add to your faith goodness; and to goodness, knowledge; and to knowledge, self-control; and to self-control, perseverance; and to perseverance, godliness; and to godliness, mutual affection; and to mutual affection, love. For if you possess these qualities in increasing measure, they will keep you from being ineffective and unproductive in your knowledge of our Lord Jesus Christ. But whoever does not have them is nearsighted and blind, forgetting that they have been cleansed from their past sins. Therefore, my brothers and sisters, make every effort to confirm your calling and election. For if you do these things, you will never stumble, and you will receive a rich welcome into the eternal kingdom of our Lord and Savior Jesus Christ.*

2 Peter 1:3–11

A lot more is expected in the Christian life than some believers may think. While it *is* by grace through faith in Christ that you are saved (Eph. 2:8), salvation is only the beginning of your new life in Christ.

Peter encourages believers to add to their faith. You can and should add goodness to your faith. To that goodness, you can add knowledge. To your knowledge, add self-control. To your self-control, add perseverance. (You'll need it for your discipline!) To your perseverance, add godliness. To your godly behavior, add mutual affection. And to your mutual affection for one another, add love.

What point is Peter trying to make with this list of everything you need to add to your faith? If these qualities increase, you'll be effective. You'll be productive. You'll come to know Jesus Christ as Lord in a new way.

As you strengthen your faith while increasing in these qualities, you'll confirm your calling in Christ. You'll walk in step with the Spirit. And best yet?

You'll be welcomed into Jesus Christ's eternal kingdom. You won't try to break in. You won't knock and knock to no avail. You'll be richly welcomed.

You and I can't begin to imagine what a rich welcome into heaven might entail. We can't wrap our minds around the sights, sounds, and sensations to be experienced. But it's coming to those who have been called by His glory and goodness. You don't know the details of the rich welcome that awaits you, and that's okay. If Jesus is your Lord and leader, your Savior and shepherd, you'll find out.

In the meantime, we have an opportunity to offer rich welcomes to our own guests. If hospitality is your desire or strength, keep in mind that the welcome you give often can set the tone for your guests' entire visit and stay.

Sometimes hosts simply can't devote much time or energy to a visit. But attentive hosts make welcoming their guests a priority. They may greet with a hug, help bring luggage into the home, or serve some special food or drink to their weary guests. Instead of guests walking into a home filled with chaos, candles may be lit and music may be playing.

It takes only a little extra effort and attention to detail to turn a welcome from forgettable to fantastic. That effort and attention will be something your guests truly appreciate.

*Lord Almighty, I know I still have Your work to do here on earth. But when I think about the rich welcome You're preparing, I can hardly wait to experience it and worship You. Please help me learn from You. Help me prepare a rich welcome for my guests. While it won't begin to compare with Your welcome, I want to be a thoughtful and kind host. I want my guests to feel like they're wanted at my home. Help me to be a gracious and thoughtful host as a way to glorify You. In Jesus' name I pray, amen.*

## Think It Over

- What was the most disappointing welcome you've ever received?
- What is the best welcome you've ever received?
- What could you do to make people feel special as you welcome them into your home?

## *Put It into Practice*

- Now that you've thought about what you could do to make someone feel special in your home, make a short list of your ideas. Keep it in a location with a few hospitality necessities so that the next time you invite company over, you can get the special touches ready in a hurry.

## *Home Work*

Depending on where you plan to host guests outside of your home—whether it's outdoor spaces at your home or public places—corral seating for you and your guests. This might include chairs, collapsible seats, camp chairs, card tables, TV trays, tablecloths or large blankets that can be used for picnics. Whatever will make your seating and eating easier, gather it now so that you're ready for outdoor, on-the-go get-togethers.

# Conclusion

After every hosting opportunity, you have a chance to say goodbye. Saying goodbye isn't always easy or quick, especially if hugs are involved and people want to sneak in last-minute conversations and meaningful sentiments before they go.

Once guests finally leave, though, your hospitality isn't over. Just like with anything else in your home, you're not completely done until things are picked up, cleaned up, and put away. Cleaning up after your guests may be quick, or it might take a while. Your home might have stayed fairly clean, and all you need to tend to is a stack of dirty dishes. Maybe you need to put party supplies away, or extra seats. Use this time of cleaning up to process everything you experienced during your time with your guests. Whether you're putting things away or taking care of dishes, it's a perfect time to reflect on what just happened. What bits and pieces of your conversations do you remember? What made you laugh? What touched your heart? What do you need to pray about?

By now, you already know that preparing for guests can take a lot of time, thought, and energy. Anticipating your guests can be a lot of fun. Actually spending time with your guests is what hospitality is all about! But afterward, don't be so quick to move on. Linger on what went really well. Consider what you could change the next time you host. And most of all, enjoy what just happened. Not only were you obedient to the biblical call to practice hospitality but your interaction with your guests was also truly special. You'll never get these moments back again. Sometimes, you may never see your guests face to face again on this side of heaven.

Just like the end of a visit, *our* time together is coming to an end. As you've read through the past fifty-two devotions, hopefully you've learned a little about opening your home to welcome others—and you've done it! More than the act of welcoming others though, hopefully you've pondered God's heart and intention behind hospitality. You've learned how and why you should care for guests with your welcome. Knowing that hospitality includes a fair amount of work that needs to be practiced, keep in mind that welcoming others extends beyond people you're most comfortable with. Invite strangers and outsiders, the marginalized, and your neighbors. Don't forget that even when surprises and snafus may come with your hospitality efforts, you'll still be able to create unforgettable events and minister to your guests both physically and spiritually in very meaningful ways.

Now that you have a better understanding of what hospitality should look like and how it can change the lives of you and your guests, may the biblical call to open your home change both your perspective and your practice. As you begin to welcome guests into your life and open your home, may the Lord continue to do a good work. Thank Him for the ways He alone can do unexpected, mighty feats as you partner together with Him in hospitality. And continue to trust Him as you love others well and open the door to your welcoming home.

# *About the Author*

Hilary Bernstein has worked as a professional journalist, editor, blogger, and author for twenty-five years. Through her blog HilaryBernstein.com, Hilary has helped thousands of Christian women transform their homes into havens.

In any spare time, Hilary and her husband, teen son, and teen daughter love hosting family and friends in their northeast Ohio home.

Currently leading more than 1,000 women as the Women's Ministry Director at The Chapel in Green, Ohio, Hilary teaches the Bible to women at her church each week. She has gathered women of all ages to study the Bible in small groups in a variety of settings for the past twenty-eight years.

Hilary began blogging in 2011, first with *Accidentally Green*, then with *Home To A Haven*. In the past, she contributed monthly blog posts to both *The Humbled Homemaker* and *Keeper of the Home* and spoke at Homemaking Ministries' online conference for five years.

She's written or cowritten twelve devotional books. Her latest book, *The Tension of Tidy*, was released in the fall of 2024.

Before blogging, Hilary was a columnist and editor of the lifestyle section of *The Gazette*, a daily newspaper in Medina, Ohio. During her ten years as editor, she wrote hundreds of articles about family, home, food, travel, and entertainment and was awarded second place as the Associated Press Best Columnist in Ohio. Previously, she was employed as a staff writer at *Christian Mission* magazine in Charlottesville, Virginia.

She earned a Bachelor of Arts in Journalism, *cum laude*, from Otterbein University in 1998. During college, Hilary was an editorial intern at *Release* magazine in Nashville, Tennessee, and *Worldwide Challenge* magazine, based out of Cru's world headquarters in Orlando, Florida. Twenty-seven years later, her *Worldwide Challenge* article, "Tending Our Talents," is still used in Cru's staff training materials.

# Scripture Index

**Romans**
12:9-13 – Devotion 14
12:18-21 – Devotion 16
15:5-7 – Devotion 49
16:23 – Devotion 18

**2 Corinthians**
12:9 – Devotion 36

**Galatians**
1:10 – Devotion 37
4:13-14 – Devotion 31

**Ephesians**
2:17-22 – Devotion 9

**Philippians**
4:6-7 – Devotion 39

**Colossians**
3:23-24 – Devotion 41

**1 Thessalonians**
1:4-6 – Devotion 7
2:8 – Devotion 7

**1 Timothy**
5:9-10 – Devotion 43

**Philemon**
15-18 – Devotion 35
22 – Devotion 34

**Hebrews**
10:24-25 – Devotion 6
13:1-2 – Devotion 13
13:15-16 – Devotion 38

**1 Peter**
1:22 – Devotion 8
4:8-9 – Devotion 8

**2 Peter**
1:3-11 – Devotion 52